"The Sum of Grief perfectly captures all of the love, longing, loss, and confusion that comes with losing a mother during the teenage years. Jessica Shannon's exploration of Grief Math is one of the best I've encountered, showing us how the loss of a mother when you're young can radiate forward in consistently new and unexpected ways. This is a beautiful book."

"Grief bends time in the most curious way. As a fellow member of "the worst club you never want to join," I met Jessica at a chaplain's conference less than a year after my own mother, a fellow Deborah, died far too soon. In The Sum of Grief, Shannon, a pediatric chaplain spiritual play expert, explores the sacred and unsettling moment when the living reach the age their parent never passed. Drawing on her own loss and years of compassionate ministry with children and families, she names the existential questions that surface for the bereaved at this threshold. This book is a wise and tender companion for anyone learning to live with this peculiar arithmetic. As one who has benefited from her companionship along this journey, I am deeply grateful and delighted to see her insight shared with the wider world."

The Sum
of Grief

The Sum of Grief

A Daughter's Memoir

Jessica Shannon

London · New Delhi · New York

PUBLISHED BY

Sūtra House Publishing · www.sutrahouse.com

The Sum of Grief: A Daughter's Memoir © 2026 Jessica Shannon

MEMOIR DISCLAIMER

This is a work of memoir. Events, conversations, and details reflect the author's memory and experience over time. Some names and identifying characteristics have been changed to protect individual privacy. The opinions and interpretations are the author's own.

CREDITS

Book Design — Sūtra House Creative

Cover Design — Eduarda Bittencourt

Printed in the United States of America

10 9 8 7 6 5 4 3 2 1

· *First Edition*

LIBRARY OF CONGRESS CATALOGING-IN-PUBLICATION DATA

Shannon, Jessica, author.
 The Sum Of Grief: A Daughter's Memoir / Jessica Shannon.
 First edition. | Houston, TX : Sūtra House Publishing, 2026.
 LCCN 2026908374
 ISBN 978-1-972806-00-5 (paperback)
 ISBN 978-1-972806-02-9 (hardcover)
 ISBN 978-1-972806-01-2 (ebook)
 Subjects: | Shannon, Jessica — Mental health. | Mothers — Death — Psychological aspects. | Grief. | Bereavement — Psychological aspects. | Motherless families. | Children and death. | Chaplains — United States — Biography.
 Classification: LCC BF575.G7 S53 2026 | DDC 155.9/37 — dc23/eng/20260401

To my mom...

I wish you were here, even if that would mean I wouldn't know enough about grief to write a book about it.

Introduction

I T WOULD NOT BE AN EXAGGERATION to say that I often draw the short straw in pretty much every category of life. That's how it feels, and I never dismiss or minimize people's feelings, including my own. I've survived it all, though, and, for most of my career, I've been helping other people survive heavy things, too. The biggest thing I've survived is becoming a motherless daughter at a young age.

Anytime someone I know loses their mother, I welcome them "into the worst club you never wanted to join." It's absolutely a club, and none of us asked for it. Being a motherless daughter isn't a choice, but it's a big part of who I am and the lens through which I view the world.

As a chaplain, I address being a motherless daughter differently — we never share our own stories — but the sentiment is still there. Being a motherless daughter creates an immediate connection to fellow club members. My ears perk up when I hear someone mention they lost their mom. It's like hearing someone speak French in Houston, seeing a woman in riding boots and breeches out running errands, or spotting someone wearing a shirt from their favorite Premier League club — I want to find a way to chat with them. We have all been tasked with navigating life without the person who gave us life. And we're making it.

If you haven't lost your mom, the idea of it sounds terrible. Let me tell you, it's worse than it sounds. The first few years after my mom's death, if I heard anyone complaining about their mom, I wanted to scream at them. "Don't you know how lucky you are?" "Oh, poor you! Your mom calls too much!" "Shut up! Who cares that she buys you the ugliest sweaters! She is here to buy you the sweater! Buy her something amazing, because you can!" I'd rather have her here and be irritated by her than not have her here. I'd give anything to wrap her in one of those tight hugs — the kind that made her cringe and smile at the same time, where she'd say, "You hug just like your dad! I can't breathe!" And she'd laugh as soon as I let go. She was tiny, and I loved ambushing her with them.

Debra Shannon died on December 12, 1998. She was 44, and I was 17. It was two weeks before Christmas during my senior year of high school. Her death changed who I was, who I am, and who I would become. It has impacted friendships, relationships, careers, my sense of self-worth, increased my empathy for animals and people, built an unshakeable belief that grief deserves to be discussed more openly, and, whether I know it or not, every decision I make. I would benefit immensely from her counsel, and I often imagine her sitting cross-legged on the futon in our game room and sharing her wisdom. There's no doubt that we would enjoy cups of tea and still ride together. We'd travel, and she'd still steal my shoes and hide them beneath hers. My shoes were one size up from hers, and she could wear mine while I couldn't fit into hers. She wore a size 5.5 women's shoe, and she thought she was so sneaky, wearing kids' Cole Haan loafers at half the price of a comparable women's pair.

Her death has led me to feel lonelier than I could have anticipated. All these years later, I still feel a dark cloud that keeps me from fully relating to my peers who have mothers. Fear, uncertainty, abandonment, and sadness have been constant. At the same time, I love more deeply, because she did. I advocate for children and animals, because no one should be without a voice or a helper. Being a motherless daughter is part of my identity. Her death changed everything, and my life turned accordingly. There's a clear before and after. Death alters how we move through the world, and that's especially true for those who experience loss as children or adolescents.

In some form, this book has lived in me since she died. It is full of stories I've shared or wished people had asked to hear. Maybe I've been afraid to tell some of them, for two reasons: first, chaplains are trained not to be vulnerable but rather to use their story to guide others in being vulnerable; and second, people tend to give you a look that says, "Haven't you gotten over that yet?" Only someone who hasn't lost someone close, especially a parent when they were both young, would believe that there's an end to grief — but goodness if it isn't said to me in various ways. Questions like these add shame to grief.

You're coming with me on a journey through grief math to see how I've viewed the world as a motherless daughter, and I wrote this throughout 2025, as my final grief math equation played itself out. Thank you for giving me the space to share. For years, I've comforted people by telling them that their story matters. My story matters, too.

This is my grief memoir, and one thing I know: we write the book we need to read. After reading countless grief books from a chaplain's lens and a motherless daughter's lens, this is the book I want to read. For years, I scoured the shelves at bookstores both online and in person to find a book that fully validated my experience, and it seems the only way for that to happen was to write it myself. You'll learn later that there is a book that made me feel seen and not alone, and, for that, I'm thankful. This book, however, is the one I needed in different ways. I hope you feel both the joy and the sorrow in it, and I hope it validates your own experience, or helps you hold someone in yours a little better.

I don't want to tell you

when they died.

If it wasn't yesterday

will you expect me to

be less broken

If you know it's been a month, a year, a decade,

if it was a lifetime ago,

will you expect my grief to be a whisper

and no longer a scream?

— SARA RIAN

The End is Near

I'VE KNOWN MY LIFE EXPECTANCY for over 20 years. Perhaps I haven't always known the exact months and years, but since I was a teenager, I knew there was little chance I'd live past 44. Is that logical? Not really, but there isn't much logic involved with grief, especially grief that began at age 17. Grief doesn't always make sense, but it's a beautiful expression of love, regardless of what you want. When we grieve who our loved one was and what we miss about them, we continue a relationship with them. What does make sense to me is the inevitable grief math that so many people admit to doing after a parent dies young. For 27 years, and certainly throughout 2025, I believed that my final grief math answer would be 44 years, 9 months, and 6 days, but there was a lot of math that led to that result.

But here I am. Facing the last year of my life, because I can't see past 44. I have no genetic model of a woman past that age. I hated every math class from elementary school through that one required math credit in college, but the headaches from geometry and algebra don't compare to the pain of figuring out the day you'll die simply because that's how long your mom lived.

The year I turn the age my mom died has been on my mind for a couple of years. It's been on the horizon, and now it's here. It really feels like the end for me, and it's comforting and validating to know that others have felt this way, too. Despite that comfort and validation, I still can't convince myself this isn't the year I'll die. It feels like 9 months and 6 days of a bucket list, and perhaps that's how I'll treat it.

We're never the same after profound losses. Even within a family, each individual griever responds differently to the same loss. One family member may openly reflect on their loved one periodically while thinking about them all the time. Another may rarely utter their name. Another person may grieve by seeking opportunities for storytelling, celebrating the life of the deceased, and speaking openly about how that loss has shaped them. I am the latter, and that's been my method of coping since her death. I'm always looking for a moment to tell a story or share an anecdote about my mom that keeps her present with me while letting people around me know how lucky I was to be her daughter for 17 years. My hope is that my way of grieving will help this difficult year feel less frightening and more joyful, more reflective.

I am the only daughter in my family, and losing a mother young leaves lifelong marks on a daughter. Being a motherless daughter has become part of my identity, and the further I am from the loss, the more the motherless part is felt. The moment fellow motherless daughters meet each other, we feel a connection. It's one of the few times that someone saying "I know how you feel" is remotely comforting. Most of the time, that's one of those statements that makes you want to scream, "No, you don't!" while giving them a tight smile instead.

Traumatic events at a young age don't simply require you to grow up faster. Experiencing the heavy parts of life earlier creates a barrier between you and other people your age. It always felt like other kids were staring at me as if there was a unicorn horn protruding from my forehead, and it can still feel that way sometimes. There was fascination but also apprehension. My freshman year of college began eight months after my mom's death, and I could talk about death and trauma with ease by then — and honestly, talking casually about her death helped me cope. I remember making a sarcastic comment about my mom at lunch during freshman orientation that appalled a classmate. It was a simple comment about my mom sometimes being mean. Name a teenage girl who wouldn't say the same thing. I'll wait. Girls with mothers say those comments freely, but a girl without a mother? Gasp! How dare I! I never felt safe around that classmate the entire four years we were in rural Virginia, because of that moment in the cafeteria before our college careers officially started. Bereaved children and adolescents need to feel safe to grieve, laugh, and be heard.

I have always paid attention to the same awkward silences and odd responses people have when they learn my mom died. This year, I'm unsettling people even more when I drop the "I'm turning the age my mom was when she died" line. There are a handful of responses to that. 1. Silence, followed by a subject change. This is a telling sign that you're uncomfortable, and that you're putting your comfort over being supportive. It tells us who can show up and who can't. 2. If they, or someone close to them, was in a similar situation, they might say, "I remember how hard it was for my dad when he reached the day his dad died." That one shows sympathy. 3. Some will have a follow-up question about how this big birthday makes me feel. This response shows both empathy and curiosity. It's my favorite. It makes me feel seen and heard, and that is incredibly powerful. It's also rare.

When someone asks about this looming milestone, they give me the opportunity to explain grief math. The curious ones are fascinated and often go on to reach out to friends who lost a parent when they were young. I feel safer explaining what a frightening year of uncertainty this is. It can help them understand how common it is to feel lost in this situation. We wonder how to navigate the years our parent never lived to see — years we must face without their example. That feels like the end.

People who are grieving, regardless of how long ago the death was, become used to awkward silences, tilted heads and furrowed brows, and well-meaning statements that land as hurtful. Occasionally, someone will ask me about my mom's life or death. Both are part of her story as well as mine. Like anyone who has lost someone close to them, it is incredibly meaningful when someone says her name and asks about her. To understand who she was, how she died, and how her death has shaped me is to make meaning of the loss.

She was Deb to some, Debbie to others, and Debra to a few. She was "Bee" to my dad. She was "Mom" to Nate and me. Her name was Debra Shannon, and I'm her daughter.

II

Grief Math

MY MOM LIVED 44 YEARS, 9 months, and 6 days. I will live 44 years, 9 months, and 6 days. I reach that age this year. It might be illogical, especially to someone who hasn't been in this spot, but it's how it feels.

It took some special math to know how long I would live. I've hated math as long as I can remember. Walking to math class, I'd feel a tightness in my chest. I felt stupid and judged in those classes, as opposed to French and literature, where I felt empowered, intelligent, and creative.

Grief math, however, is easy and oftentimes comforting. It is a common coping skill among people who lost a parent or sibling when they were young.

To be honest, I thought I had coined the term "grief math" until hearing Stephen Colbert chat with Anderson Cooper on Cooper's grief podcast, "All There Is." Cooper started the podcast after his mother's death forced him to face the grief he'd long carried over his father and his brother, who died by suicide. In Cooper's words, he "muted that part" of his life and was now processing his cumulative grief with grace, curiosity, and love. He had learned that grief isn't linear, and that cumulative grief occurs when our losses stack on top of each other — new losses triggering feelings from old ones.

Both Colbert and Cooper shared the grief math they did, and I realized how normal this type of math is for people who lost a parent when they were young. Colbert was 10 years old when his dad and two of his brothers died in a plane crash. He stated that he would count the years until his kids would turn 10 and assume he'd die when they each turned 10, starting with the oldest. He reflected on doing what he referred to as "that horrible math," which is grief math. He didn't know what it was like for a child past the age of ten to have a father, and he was worried about each of his children as they turned that age. He did also grief math as he approached 53 - his dad's age at the time of his death.

When he turned 53, he wondered what his dad would do on that day. He then traveled around the country to see each of his children without telling them why, and then he went to Washington, D.C. where most of his living siblings lived. Over dinner, they asked the purpose of his visit. He replied, "Well, on Friday, I turned 53 years, and then the people around the table said, 'and 274 days old?' They had done the math, too...in their own lives on that day."

Grief math is how grievers track time since a loss, or toward a specific milestone or age that connects us to the person who died. It's a coping tool that gives us some sense of control, and a common way to calculate our own mortality based on when our loved one died. It's how we measure something that seems impossible to measure: our loss. There are both stages and variations to this type of math.

The variations of grief math are full of milestones, death anniversaries, and other significant days on our grief calendar. We may add up the hours, days, and months since they've been gone to validate the loss and make sense of it. We mark achievements they missed and find our own ways to carry the anniversary of their death. We ask ourselves questions — "How old would she be now?" and "How many of my birthdays have they missed?" We wonder when we will be their age at the time of their death, and we figure it out to the day. The math isn't all doom and gloom. Some equations are sad, for sure. Some calculations, however, can give us hope that we are surviving without them. We'd rather we didn't have to, but we are grasping a life without them and letting grief be our companion rather than an enemy. Early in my grief, I dove into grief math as if it were the safe space I needed, guiding me through a time when I was working through life and loss alone, and very young. It kept me steady and helped me navigate my future without a mother, and I divided grief math into stages.

The first overall stage of grief math is calculating how many years we live with our mother or father versus how many years without them. We'll stick with my personal math rather than hypothetical examples. Math teachers famously ask their students to show their work, and I fumbled every step of the way, regardless of the type of math we were studying. I mastered grief math, however, without trying. I was 17 when she died. The first stage told me that for the next 16 years, I had lived with a mother longer than without one.

I lived the first 17 years of my life with a mother. Memories of her were fresh, vivid, and real — but after about a year, I couldn't remember the sound of her voice or her laughter. I could visualize her talking, but it was like she was on mute. That bright smile of hers stayed with me, though. In a letter, a friend of hers described her: "Your mom was a tiny lady with a giant heart. She loved life, she was crazy about her family." Kids at my school often commented on her smile and how genuinely kind she was. I was learning to make sense of being a motherless daughter. I remember this phase feeling like I was standing at the edge of a cliff. Behind me was the life of a daughter who had a mom who rode horses, thought it was okay to reuse a tea bag (it's not), and went on TJ Maxx shopping sprees when she was stressed about hosting. My brother and I once played a game where we pointed at random things around the house — a giant bowl, a teal and cream rug — and had to name which panic-hosting occasion Mom had bought each one for. Like me, my mom was short. We're both under 5 feet tall, but unfortunately I didn't inherit her metabolism. She only surpassed 100 pounds twice in her life, and those were the two times she was pregnant. She was teeny, but the love radiating from her was massive. I was facing an unknown that felt as big as the joy and love my mom gave out to everyone she met, and I couldn't see what was before me without her. It seemed dark, and as though I'd have to navigate it all on my own. Even when surrounded by people, I felt isolated.

From age 17 to 34, her death felt real, but I was still on the beautiful, manageable, habitable land that led to the cliff. It was almost as if there were still opportunities to wake up from the nightmare and find her downstairs, drawing our greyhound in his bed in front of the fireplace, or giggling that he had stolen some more Tupperware and was cuddling it. I had lived with her most of my life. The tears and loneliness were heaviest in this part of grief math, but some hope remained. Her voice may have drifted from my memory, but her advice still stuck with me. I remembered having a mom, even if she was fading. When people told stories about their moms, I would try to keep the conversations anchored to our childhood through high school, because I could relate to having a mom during those seasons of life. I didn't have any stories about us after my first semester of senior year. The last picture we took together was at my high school homecoming. I was Student Council President, and Mom led the Senior Moms group and was planning our prom. Homecoming was held at the Great Southwest Equestrian Center, where our horse was boarded and our shows were held. While many high schools have themes for their dances, my little international school took the themes seriously — beyond the decorations. Our theme that year was something about heroes in movies. Because of that, the last picture my mom and I took together looks a bit odd. She's beaming in her classic pixie cut and a navy ensemble — a tank top and full-length skirt — and I'm dressed as Princess Leia in a costume she sewed.

During the first stage of grief math, if I felt angry, sad, or abandoned, I would think, "I had her most of my life" to comfort myself. Until I was 34, that was true. My 34th birthday felt sad and ominous, and my grief felt fresh again. The second stage of grief math is the shortest — the 50/50 mark. Every day after that, the scales shifted in a devastating way.

If we get completely technical, the second stage lasts just one day. When I was 34 years, 9 months, and 6 days old, I had lived 17 years with her and 17 years without. At that point, however, I only focused on whole years and didn't concern myself with the days and months. I felt the shift when I turned 34 — half my life with a mother, half without. Counting down to an exact day came later. This was the first time I hated the result of this math problem. It was real now.

In the first 17 years without her, I graduated from high school, college, and graduate school, completed five units of Clinical Pastoral Education (CPE) to become a chaplain, faced some relationship and career highs and lows, traveled to seven countries — some repeats, some new — and lived in three different states. I also lost my beloved paternal grandparents, two dogs, two cats, and the horse I shared with Mom, and gained four dogs, including my soulmate pet. She missed all of it. She wasn't there to celebrate any accomplishments or guide me through the never-ending obstacles I seemed to face. The math was beginning to look like the math I loathed in school. I often danced with failing math every semester yet somehow ended up with a low B by the end of the grading period. Math was betraying me again.

After that brief 50/50 mark, I was motherless longer than I had a mother. It was all downhill. This is the stage where you feel fully motherless or fatherless. It was strange. I felt so alone and scared, and there was rarely anyone I could be completely honest with about how I felt — on those occasions when I even had words for it. Her death felt final again. Children who lose a parent or sibling often begin their grief again at each new stage of life, as they face milestones, aging, and major decisions without their parent. Like other bereaved kids, I did this. I do this. There was a heaviness when I realized that my life without a mother was forever longer than my life with the mother who taught me to treat every human and animal with compassion and respect.

It seemed like my grief math work was going to be covered in red pen for the rest of my life. We all know that sinking feeling when your test is handed back to you, covered in red. But this time, no amount of studying or time with a tutor would improve the answer to the next grief math question. I was motherless. The math wasn't mathing. I hated it. Most days, it felt as though I never had a mother unless I looked at pictures. Even then, she seemed like a dream we'd made up.

She loved the band The Cure. My brother and I each went through phases of listening to their CDs on repeat, and I still periodically put their whole discography on shuffle on Apple Music. Mom was energized when they were playing on the living room stereo or in the car. She took my friend and me to see them, and the majority of the audience was dressed up like Robert Smith with extravagant makeup and all-black clothes. She lamented that we hadn't done the same, and I couldn't decide if that was a cool or an embarrassing thing for her to say as I imagined my mom dressed like Robert Smith. Given that she is only real to me in photographs, I'm led to a verse of one of their songs called "Pictures of You." The song beautifully describes how it feels to look at pictures of someone significant in your life and feel as though all you have left of them are the photos. Mom loved that song, as do I. We would sing it together, but now the lyrics feel like my reality.

At this stage in my life, the answer to grief math was heartbreaking. Was she even real? Were my memories of her real? I only had snapshots of her by then. It truly felt like not having a mom was as much a part of who I was as being an equestrian and French speaker, and I had no idea who I would be, or what my life would look like, if she had lived.

The final two parts of the grief math problem are the hardest to comprehend for people who haven't needed to do this math — but all too familiar for everyone in our club, and they arrive one right after the other. First, we turn the age our parent was when they died. It is daunting.

For me, this part of grief math lasts 9 months and 6 days. I have been dreading this stage since year one, and it's here. The penultimate grief math problem lasts the day of my 44th birthday and the following 9 months and 6 days.

With every headache, every doctor's appointment, every physical pain, I wonder if I will die. I'm not alone in this. Countless adults who lost a parent as children encounter this phase of grief math the same way. It's as if we can't see past this year — there is a looming wall blocking us from seeing beyond it or even hoping for a future. We aren't sure how to navigate life without a guide for how those years look. I'm thankful Stephen Colbert and Anderson Cooper named this feeling on such a public platform, and I am certain many young grievers related to it just as I did.

I have always been a planner, a daydreamer, a future thinker. This year, however, I cannot think a few days in advance, let alone to mid-December or 2026. I don't know what life looks like past 44 without my mom's example. It doesn't matter how many people, particularly women, I have known who are 45 and over. None of them are my mother. There seems to be no future past this year for me. This honestly feels like the year I will die.

We aren't quite finished with our grief math when we turn the age our parent was when they died. There is one more answer to the problem. Even when it feels very final and uncertain, we hopefully live longer than our parent did.

That's the final equation. One day I will be the exact age she was when she died: 44 years, 9 months, and 6 days. The next day, I will be 44 years, 9 months, and 7 days. That will be the day I outlive my mother.

Surpassing the age your mom died is like acing a calculus test when you regularly use a calculator to figure out 12 minus 1. It is disorienting to be older than your mom when you're still young. How can I be older than my mom? It doesn't make sense. Who is your guide? What does the future look like? There is no model to tell you how to tackle aging, no one to gab with on a mother-daughter trail ride.

These grief math stages helped me cope through storytelling, connection, and articulating complex feelings. With each phase, my identity as a daughter held by a mother's love faded a little more. I added up the days, months, and years without her and the number of holidays she missed. I calculated how long it would be until I was her age when she died, and that number loomed like it was my final number, too. My world felt out of control, lonely, and unpredictable, but I could lean on grief math. For the first time in my life, math made sense. It helped me understand grief in all its complexities. Grief didn't feel so much like a problem to solve but rather an expression of love, and I was prepared to show my work.

III

No Time for Goodbye

LIFE IS A MIX OF JOY and sorrow — and sometimes those feelings arrive simultaneously, grief coexisting with gratitude and happiness. I immensely value the people who have sat with me in both. My grief shaped me, and I'm certain it steered me toward a helping profession — though I always imagined that would mean living in Europe in some way. My family assumed so, too. The word "chaplain" wasn't even in my vocabulary.

My family hosted exchange students every year from middle school on, my brother and I attended an international school, and we were both exchange students ourselves. Stepping into other people's worlds came naturally to me at an early age. I made friends with international kids long before attending the international school and enjoyed learning about their cultures while helping them feel at home. I was drawn to people who came with a story and a culture drastically different from my own.

My mom loved to ask kids about their language's onomatopoeia. I don't remember how she smelled or how her voice sounded, but I will never forget the excitement and enthusiasm she had when meeting people of other cultures. She passed that on to both my brother and me. She felt it broke the ice to hear kids share how a cow moos in Norwegian, French, Spanish, German, and Vietnamese. As a teenager, this embarrassed me to no end, but now I see what a loving thing it was for my mom to ask my friends, "What does a cow say in Swedish?" Her curiosity told others they mattered and their culture was worth knowing. My parents encouraged us to dive into other people's worlds — to connect and become more well-rounded people. My dad taught us through cooking. My mom taught us through openness, vulnerability, and a deep interest in others. That foundation of connecting with people where they were laid the groundwork for who I am as a chaplain and as a woman. When other chaplains and healthcare workers struggle to navigate other cultures, I tend to thrive. This was part of the joy of life for me.

Then death came and didn't want to leave.

In the summer of 1998, my dad's mom had a stroke. Emily Shannon, who we called "Beebaw," had already survived polio in her childhood, and numerous other ailments. My mom often encouraged us to look to her to learn what it meant to be resilient. If we complained about something trivial or being too tired to clean our rooms, she'd name a disease or condition my paternal grandmother had endured, then say, "And you never see her complaining!" That may have been a bit of gaslighting sprinkled with encouragement, but the point about her powering through every obstacle was not missed. Nothing shook my grandmother. She lived by faith and loved others through magnificent baking, making custom Christmas bow ties for every man in her church, and a smile that lit up her perfect dining room. Her Christian faith was more visible in her actions than anyone else I've ever met, and that remains true more than 20 years after her death. We visited her that summer in Ohio while my French exchange student joined us on an East Coast college tour to help me plan for my future.

Beebaw was determined to walk again after her stroke, and it shook me to see her looking so vulnerable. I spoke to her more defiantly than I ever had before — we were always instructed to treat her with the utmost respect, as though speaking to the Dowager Countess of Grantham. She stood behind a walker and hadn't yet taken a step. In a shockingly rude tone, I said, "I'm not going to push you around Ireland in a wheelchair. You need to be able to walk." Whoa. My mom and my grandmother's physical therapist froze. I wanted to vomit. I wanted to hit rewind and not speak to her so forcefully. What did my grandmother do? She took her first steps since her stroke, and she strolled toward me with a clear goal.

Long before her stroke, I had told her that Mom and I would love to explore Ireland with her and her sister. I'm not sure how I discovered that both she and her sister wanted to visit Ireland as tourists, but I shared their dream with my mom. My mom lit up and quickly became determined that we would take a girls' trip to Ireland. The four of us would explore as much as my grandmother's body would allow, and my mom suggested that she and I would ride horses while we were there. Apparently, even the idea of that trip had sparked something in my grandmother that I was unaware of until I told her I had no intention of pushing her in a wheelchair down any cobblestone streets. I don't know where that came from, but it was probably the only time I could get away with speaking to her that way. It worked. The trip was all the bait she needed. Joy came in the sorrow of her stroke, and there was hope.

Not long before Thanksgiving of that same year, my mom said we should go to Ohio for Thanksgiving. We hadn't celebrated Thanksgiving at my dad's parents' house since we moved to Texas in 1991. The three-day holiday didn't give us enough time to justify flying four people north, nor was it long enough to merit a road trip. We celebrated most Thanksgivings in Houston and visited grandparents at Christmas or in the summer instead. Thanksgiving 1998 was a different story. Because of my grandmother's stroke, my mom declared we needed to figure out a way for us all to be in Ohio. My brother was two and a half hours away at Carnegie Mellon University in Pittsburgh, and that only required Mom, Dad, and me to make the cross-country trip. I vividly remember her saying, "This could be our last Thanksgiving together." She never said why, but her message was clear. Mom didn't say Beebaw's name, but we knew what she meant. She was right that it would be our last Thanksgiving together, but she was wrong about the person who would leave us.

My mom had been complaining of headaches before Thanksgiving, but headaches were not unusual in our house, particularly for me. I still have them almost daily when I wake up. The humidity of Houston was tough on our sinuses. She was a nurse turned medical malpractice paralegal, and her headaches did not alarm her. If they didn't concern her, why would they worry anyone else in the family?

She was incredibly healthy. She rode horses with me, ate well but not obnoxiously so, and she went on three-mile runs a few times per week. My dad bought her a special outfit to run in the snow along Lake Erie to keep up her activity while we were in Ohio. She went for a run in her fleece suit and was gone for a long time — far longer than usual — and we wondered where she was. My parents grew up in that neighborhood, which meant there was no way she was lost. Their childhood homes were three blocks apart, and their families still lived in those houses. It was well before people had cell phones except for hefty ones that stayed in the car. Although we all wondered where she was, we did nothing about it except remark that she'd been gone a bit long. She finally returned and reported having to sit down on the curb, struggling to breathe. Seventeen-year-old me thought she was being dramatic and went upstairs while she recounted her panic with my dad. I remember rolling my eyes as I climbed the stairs, and I've carried a lot of guilt about those few seconds over the years.

Five days later, we were back in Houston, and I was driving home from my dreaded SAT prep course after school. The cell phone — well, car phone — rang. It was my brother. He was back in college in Pittsburgh, and he told me he had news but didn't want to share it while I was driving. If you're wondering why he called a phone that only belonged in a car to tell me news he refused to share while I was driving, you are thinking exactly what I was. The logic in that angered, confused, and frustrated me. After some prodding, he finally shared that Mom's headaches had worsened enough that the neighbors took her to the hospital while I was in school that day. Scans showed a brain tumor, and she was at the hospital closest to our house. It was December 1, 1998, and I was leaving on a school theatre trip to England the following day.

Snuggled together in what was probably a triage bed, Mom chatted about what they found. She told me our family doctor was making calls to get her transferred quickly to a specialty hospital. We watched a Seinfeld rerun as she explained what she knew so far. The episode was season 9's "The Burning," and her belly laugh during the banter about Christian rock stations on David Puddy's car radio will forever bring me joy. There was joy in the sorrow, and it was thanks to Jerry, Elaine, George, and Kramer. That episode remains one of my favorites, and I can see, but not hear, her laughing every time I watch it.

Mom did not accept my offer to skip my school trip and be with her. She told me my brother, Nate, had offered to come home from college early, but she wanted him to finish his exams. His 21st birthday was on the 18th, and he was, for the first time in a while, giving her free rein to plan a celebration. She loved to make even the smallest moment special, and she was incredibly excited to celebrate his big birthday. She loved birthdays, and I inherited that obsession — making sure everyone feels loved on theirs. Mom still declined his offer to come home early before the semester ended.

She wanted me to go on my trip, too. It was to be a life-changing trip that included a workshop with the Royal Shakespeare Company in Stratford-Upon-Avon with other International Baccalaureate theatre students from around the world. Because it was a school trip, we couldn't use my dad's seemingly infinite supply of air miles earned from years of worldwide work travel. She reminded me that she had canceled the local newspaper subscription and made other sacrifices to help pay for it, and she didn't want me to miss it. Off I went the next day.

We spoke on the phone a few times throughout the trip. She shared that our family doctor got her into the specialty hospital quickly. Toward the end of my England adventure, she told me the doctors believed the tumor to be benign and had scheduled surgery to remove it. My mom did not want to sit in the hospital until surgery, so she went home to spend time with my dad, our cats, our dogs, and our horse. My dad told me the two cats and two dogs followed her around the house, which was rather unusual for all four to unite. Our spirited horse also lay his head on her shoulder and wouldn't budge. He said Mom was fascinated by how still Dancer was, but it gave Dad a sinking feeling that something wasn't right. They knew something. Animals always know.

While cruising on British Airways back to Houston on December 10, my mom was in brain surgery. I am never nervous when flying. In fact, I have some of the best naps on planes. I once fell asleep on the tarmac in Houston, waiting for takeoff, and woke up on the runway in Paris. That December 10 flight, however, was horrific. It felt like it would never end, and she was all I could think of the entire 10 hours, even with the drunk, passed-out Welsh rugby fan in the aisle.

The next day, my dad and I went to see her. I don't know this for sure, but my hospital experience now leads me to believe she was in the Neuro ICU, which makes sense. She was in one bed of many in a large room with curtains separating the beds. For some reason, I decided to bring her Christmas present with me, unwrapped. My mom loved English Christmas Crackers almost as much as she loved decorations that transported you to the Cotswolds. While in Stratford-Upon-Avon, I had bought her handmade Christmas Crackers from a Christmas market, and I decided she needed to see them and not wait until December 25. She was in severe pain and wincing, but she still lit up when she saw them. Joy amid so much sorrow. She asked me to adjust the pillow beneath her post-op head, and she yelped in extreme pain when I barely touched it. It scared and confused me. I had never seen her seem so weak. I was jet-lagged and did not understand what was happening. A doctor arrived, put his arm around me, and said, "Don't you worry. She'll be riding that horse of yours in two weeks." Seventeen-year-old me felt hope and peace from his encouraging words. The chaplain in me knows it is beyond impossible for someone to ride a horse two weeks after neurosurgery. Thankfully for that doctor, teen Jessica didn't have the knowledge a clinical chaplain has. I left the hospital and went to ride our horse before napping off my jet lag.

That night, my dad said he'd be staying with Mom at the hospital. I'd be alone. He also said she didn't want me to come back to the hospital. That offended me. How could my mom not want me to see her? He said she figured she'd be home soon enough, and she didn't like me seeing her that way. It really angered me that she didn't want me to see her, and it irritated me that, as far as I knew, Dad didn't advocate for me. What kind of kid doesn't spend all day at the hospital with their mom? I will always regret not standing my ground and forcing my way into her room. I wish I had been a stubborn teenager and refused to listen to what my parents said. Even if she had slept the whole time, or it was beyond boring to sit in a sterile hospital — it wouldn't have mattered. I would never regret spending more time with my mom. I only regret giving in and losing precious minutes I'd never get back.

IV

December 12, 1998

M Y PLAN FOR SATURDAY, December 12, was to
ride my horse and spend time with Mom in
her hospital room. I was heartbroken that she
didn't want me there. Dad said he was going to be with her
all day and stay the night again. I would be on my own once
more. I asked if I could go to a concert with my best friend,
and Dad agreed. I brought the car phone along and hopped
in the backseat of my friend's rickety car — I hated carrying
a purse, but I wasn't going anywhere without it. I vividly
remember sticking the bulky phone in the back pocket of

my jeans and not being able to sit properly because it was so big. We weren't even close to the music venue when my dad called and told me to go home. The neighbors would drive me to the hospital, because Mom wasn't well. I said my best friend would drop me off. My dad insisted the neighbors bring me, and that was the right call. They were like family and needed to be there for both of us.

I was both bored and worried in the empty waiting area of the hospital. No one really told me what was going on, which left me in the dark. My dad spoke to the neighbors, and I spun in a chair. At one point, I found a small room to the side with a landline and, simply to entertain myself, called a bunch of friends and chatted with whomever answered. It's amazing how many phone numbers we knew by heart back then, and now we barely know our own. I now know that rooms like the one I found are used for having difficult conversations with families — especially when the waiting room is too busy — but we didn't need that room that night. We were the only ones there that late. In my professional role, I've held many hands, offered countless tissues, and provided a calming presence in those rooms. Hospital staff call them the "bad news room."

I have no clue how long we waited, but I remember being back in the big waiting room — about 15 feet from my dad and neighbors, still on the phone — when the doctor arrived. I told whoever was on the line that the doctor was there and hung up, but I didn't get up. I've asked myself why I stayed put, and the only thing I can think of is that neither the doctor nor my dad motioned for me to join them. The doctor's body language shut me out of the conversation. I've since learned that so much of those moments lives in how a doctor walks into a room, where they stand, who they look at. That doctor could have used some of that awareness. I watched from afar and couldn't hear a word.

My mom and I used to watch *ER* together on Thursday evenings, and we always changed the channel when the doctor gave the "we did all we could" speech to a family. I remember the first time we watched one of those scenes. She simply said something about how terrible those moments were, and for a moment I got a glimpse of her life as a nurse, years before. She simply said something about how terrible those moments were, and how she could always tell what was coming by the way the doctor on screen approached the family. Now I watch families fall apart when I enter a room with a doctor. That's never a good sign. Mom and I always switched the show back with uncanny timing, missing only the sad bit and nothing else. That night, watching from across the waiting room, I observed the doctor's body language and facial expressions. I will never forget looking to both sides of me for the remote to change the channel. Mom was gone, and I never got to say "goodbye."

A couple more friends of our family arrived, and I'm not sure who called them. It was good they were there, though. A chaplain came, too — I had never heard of a chaplain. He couldn't explain his role to me, and I wanted to know why a stranger who seemed uncomfortable and unable to explain his job to a teenager was so physically close to my dad. That's where I should be. He stayed, because my dad wanted him there. I imagine he was exactly what my dad needed, but I felt so alone — almost as though I was a burden on the night of my own mother's death. That chaplain made a profound impact on me, but not in the way he probably hoped.

That chaplain did not provide any spiritual or emotional support for me. He did give that to my dad, and for that, I'm grateful. What he did — and didn't do — for me still shapes how I work. I make sure every person in the room knows my role and why I'm there, and I make sure they feel comfortable. Because of his discomfort with a teenager, my care as a pediatric chaplain is intentionally open, loving, and clear for every age and developmental stage in the room.

As I sat off to the side, I distinctly remember watching my dad and thinking, "He'll get remarried someday." That's an odd thought to surface minutes after you learn your mom has died. My parents were high school sweethearts who met in 9th grade. Regardless, I thought it. I immediately sent up an arrow prayer: "God, give me a great mother-in-law someday." I've come to understand that what I was really asking for was someone to love me the way only a mother could. I have never found anything close to a mother's love, no matter how hard I've tried.

The first thing I said out loud was to a friend of ours from France. She was the lovely woman who connected us with the Parisian family who hosted me as an exchange student in both Paris and Île d'Yeu, and two of their kids stayed with us, including on the summer college road trip. She was also part of my mom's bucket list trip to Europe and rode horses with us. She arrived and gave me a hat she had bought my mom to wear once she started chemotherapy. Mom didn't even get to the point where chemotherapy could give her a chance at life. I told our friend, "She won't see me graduate from high school." That would be the first of many milestones Mom would miss in my life.

Between December 12, 1998, and April 2006, I lost two family dogs, both of my dad's parents, two family cats, and my horse. The dogs and Beebaw died when I was in college. We were able to say goodbye to Beebaw in a small hospice facility in Ohio, and then I went back to Virginia. My dad said I didn't need to return for the funeral and miss school. I deeply regret listening to him. His reasoning was that we had seen her and said our goodbyes — but I believe my heart and grief needed to see their church filled with people celebrating how loved she was and what an impact she had made on her community. My paternal grandfather died not long after I graduated, and I couldn't afford the plane ticket to go to his funeral. That made me sad, but it doesn't sit with me still the way missing my grandmother's service does. The family cats and my horse died nearly every other month for the first four months of 2006 — about halfway through seminary. Each of those deaths was hard in its own way. I shared my first horse with my mom. Losing him felt like losing the last piece of her that was just mine.

Every December 12 is as important on my calendar as any holiday or birthday. There is a distinct before and after December 12, 1998 — in who I am and who my family is — and the date sticks out to me as if it were in a neon font anytime it appears on a movie poster or is said on the news. That day will always be significant, and it is a constant in every grief math equation.

Quick Grief Math

MY GRIEF MATH STARTED RIGHT AWAY and was easy addition at first, even for me. It went like this:

1 day after her diagnosis, I left for a school trip in England.

9 days after her diagnosis, she had neurosurgery while I flew back to Houston.

10 days after her diagnosis, I spoke to her for the last time.

11 days after her diagnosis, she was dead.

All of it traced from the discovery of Mom's brain tumor to a significant day in those first twelve days of December. It mapped the last eleven days of her life like a timeline — even as grief math itself insists that grief doesn't have one.

I focused on those first grief math numbers for years. When someone asked me how long Mom was sick, I responded with either "We knew for 11 days" or "There were 11 days between diagnosis and death." Sometimes I'd add, "and I was in England for most of those days." These numbers made up the beginning of my grief story and the end of Mom's life, and they helped me make sense of things while guiding me toward a succinct way of telling it. (As a chaplain, I'm careful about using the word "sick" with children when discussing cancer or tumors — I use those words directly instead. But in telling my own story, "sick" is how it came out.)

Twenty-seven years later, I still rely on those first 12 days of December as the foundation of my grief math. From December 1–12, 1998, the math gave me terrible results, but she was still alive. The first equations were simple: count back from any specific moment to the day her brain tumor showed up on an MRI. I started tracking time around my loss immediately.

The grief math for the first year was simple, even for a girl who had severe math anxiety. On the 12th of every month, I would work out a few problems. The first: subtract December — the 12th month — from the current month to get how many months since she left me. I wanted to say out loud, "I've been motherless for 6 months," and "Mom died 8 months ago." I needed to say it for it to be real. When we calculate grief math, we are trying to hold onto our loved one and understand our loss — to keep track of the days that are obviously going to be hard, like Christmas, birthdays, Mother's Day, and Thanksgiving, as well as the ones that don't announce themselves on the calendar: personal achievements, developmental milestones, and the surprising ones — the first day at a new job, or reaching for her when picking up a horse show ribbon.

Each time I told someone the story of my loss through grief math, I felt like I had some control over the nightmare. Each time I shared the details of those dreaded days, I healed a little. If I could tell them how many days had passed between diagnosis and death, or how old she would be that year, I was still somehow hanging onto her — keeping her a part of both the big and small moments of my life. Because the story of her death mattered as much as the story of her life.

VI

Funerals Are for the Living

DECEMBER 13, 1998, WAS THE BEGINNING of a few days of blurry numbness and a lifetime of growing with grief. Neighbors and barn friends arrived to clean our house and bring food for the inevitable revolving door of guests offering condolences. I can't remember if the doorbell rang all day or if people simply let themselves in to relieve us of having to answer the door. Maybe a neighbor answered it. Those details didn't stick with me, but many did.

It wasn't long before our formal living room at the front of the house was filled with my friends. Mom always had baby gates keeping the dogs out of that room and off the nicer couches — as if she were always expecting someone to drop by and needed a nice place to entertain — but, other than my dreaded piano practice and the Christmas tree, it wasn't used much. Every other room in the house had evidence that animals were a priority. I quickly became oblivious to what was happening in the rest of the house and sat on the puffy couches Mom had picked out a few years before, surrounded by kids from Mexico, Norway, France, Scotland, Syria, England, Ecuador, Belgium, Iran, Italy, Brazil, and local Houstonians who were all my school friends. I'm not sure who started the phone tree, but it was astonishing how quickly teenagers poured into our living room to show me they cared. I soon learned that those same kids supported me more authentically than any adult in my life — despite only one of them having experienced a similar life-altering loss.

At one point, my uncle arrived with my brother. Nate had taken the first flight he could get from Pittsburgh, and my uncle picked him up from the airport. Without saying a word, I got up, and we hugged each other tighter than we ever had. Later, my high school best friend told me that moment hit him hard. He knew my brother and I had a difficult relationship, and seeing us share a moment of love and pain was poignant. It said everything about the weight of it all. My best friend and I both assumed Nate and I would become close after our shared loss — but that didn't happen, not really. It was, however, astounding to me how much that hug moved my friend. It's a hug I won't ever forget, because it was the most genuine expression of love we'd ever shared, and neither my brother nor I spoke a word.

My dad, brother, and I soon began planning Mom's funeral. We rushed every decision — partly due to the shock of her death, and partly because we had no idea how to navigate any of the steps after someone dies. We needed Mom's gift for planning and leading, but she was gone. Since 1998, in both my professional and personal lives, I've witnessed people wait weeks and even months for a memorial service. We had Mom's service two days after she died.

The first decision was a funeral home. I'm pretty sure my dad just opened the yellow pages and picked the first one under "A." Hospitals will ask families if they have a funeral home picked out, because whoever they choose comes to the hospital to pick up the body. I've been present for these conversations countless times as a chaplain — and I know that families can leave the hospital without making that decision right away. No one told us that. We felt pressured in the midst of our shock and confusion, and Dad grabbed the first one. It was, in a word, shady. She deserved far better. Thankfully, only family viewed Mom's body, and Dad chose to have her cremated, buying us more time to decide where to bury her. She hadn't shared her wishes for end of life — her prognosis, as we'd been told, was good, and there had been so little time. The service was to be held at the church where my parents and I were members.

One of the pastors of our church stopped by the house to learn more about Mom and ask what we'd like in the service. Our church was large, and, unlike our previous ones, my parents didn't have close relationships with the pastors there. I knew them better, and my mom had let me choose this church for our family. The pastor who came by had a daughter in the youth group a year younger than me. I only remember one part of the pre-service conversation, and it is not a good memory. When our pastor asked about hymns we'd like, I piped in. "Mom's favorite hymn was 'Be Thou My Vision,'" I said, with a mixture of confidence, sadness, and love. I was proud to know that. My brother told me to "be quiet." I don't believe I spoke again for the rest of the meeting. That was my contribution to the service, and I don't think the hymn made it into the order of service.

My church had two sanctuaries: a massive one and a small chapel. The small chapel comfortably sat 150 people, if I recall. That's where most memorial services were held, including Mom's. The number of people who arrived was unforgettable. The chapel was bursting with people from Mom's current and former jobs, Dad's work, the neighborhood, family who traveled from all over, horse friends, my teachers, and friends of both my brother and me. My high school must have been very empty that day — so many teachers, administrators, students, and their families were there. People were standing, unable to find a seat in the overflowing pews. Seeing that many people was one of the healing moments of early grief. I could tell she was loved. I could tell we were loved.

Funerals and memorial services are a celebration of the lost life, but they are really meant for the bereaved. They are a moment that tells us: "This is real. They're gone." After all these years, I still feel a little robbed that my one contribution wasn't in the service. I was immensely proud that Mom had told me "Be Thou My Vision" was her favorite hymn. She told me on one of our dog walks. She had never discussed hymns with me before — that was more of my paternal grandfather's territory. When she told me what that hymn meant to her, I remember thinking that maybe I needed a favorite, too. Since her death, I still can't make it through "Be Thou My Vision" without crying.

There are three moments in the service that have stuck with me. The first was my dad's cell phone ringing. Nearly everyone we knew was in that chapel, and not many people carried cell phones in 1998, which made it even more surprising. Apparently, Dad had turned it off, but someone had asked him to turn it back on to help guide someone who was lost on the way to the church. This was years before reliable GPS. I'm glad that happened, though. Those few seconds seemed to wake me up from a daze. The second moment was my brother playing cello. I remember staring at him as he played Bach, thinking there was no way I could perform anything. I even thought, "If someone set up jumps in the courtyard and said that part of the service was for Dancer and me to jump a course, I couldn't do it." I was in awe of his ability to muster that strength. It was surely an expression of grief for him.

The final memorable moment in the service was something the pastor said. For the most part, my family was not thrilled with how our church handled the service, but there was one thing he said that painted a vivid picture for me. He was quoting my dad: "Dan said, 'God loved through Deb.'" In the moment, I couldn't grasp what that really meant, but I knew it was one of the most loving statements my dad could make about his beloved wife. As the meaning of that sentence became clearer to me over the years, it became a goal of mine. I hope people can say the same about me. A couple of years before Mom died, she told me that more people will notice my actions as a Christian than my words. She said people would have a better understanding of God's love by how I loved them — and as it turned out, that's how she lived, too. I'll never forget when I went home and told her that kids at school had asked me why she was always so happy and smiling. She replied, "Simple. Jesus." She then told me, "People will learn more about Jesus by how you love them than any sermon. Love everyone. It's not hard."

When the service ended, Nate, Dad, and I walked out of the chapel. It was the first time we were truly able to see how many people were there, and it was overwhelming in the best way. A lot of people gathered at our house afterward. I remember one of my brother's friends asking me, "Who is that little lady who is making all of this about her?" According to a handful of Nate's friends, one of the older women was loudly saying odd things about my mom. Not a single story or statement she made demonstrated love for my mother on the day of her funeral. I asked them to point out this person. It was my mom's mother. That was one of the last times I ever saw her.

Nate was home for a few more weeks. In that time, we visited a few cemeteries to find a resting place for Mom's ashes. Dad had lamented that she never "felt at home anywhere." Her childhood lacked love. That's an understatement. She was treated with disdain and cruelty by her stepfather, and her mom wasn't much better. Their treatment of her ruled Ohio out as a resting place. Houston didn't feel right either. She loved everyone she met from the barn and my school and had dear friends from each of her jobs, but Houston wasn't home for her. Finally, my dad's mom offered a spot in the family plot in Sewickley, PA. My paternal grandmother loved my mom like a daughter — a fact she shared with me once, not long after Mom died. That moment of expressive sentiment was rare for her, which made it all the more meaningful. The cemetery in Sewickley was once run by my great-great-aunt's family, and we have a small section off the side of a massive hill where generations of my dad's family are buried. On a rainy November day in 1999, just eleven months after her death, we buried Mom's ashes on that plot with family friends from Pittsburgh by our side. A few years later, both of my paternal grandparents were buried alongside her. My mom had a home with them in life, and it brought me such peace to know her burial place was next to theirs. After that quiet and rainy day, I felt a weight lift. A new phase of grief could begin now that Mom's ashes were no longer waiting for a place.

———

VII

False Hope and Broken Trust

DEBRA BEDELL — HER MAIDEN NAME, one that meant nothing to her since it didn't reveal who her father was and only further ostracized her from her siblings — went to nursing school in Elyria, Ohio, after graduating from Avon Lake High School. She had long black hair that she straightened using old orange juice cans. My whole life, though, she wore it cut in a short bob or close-cropped. After becoming a nurse and marrying Dan Shannon, she practiced nursing for years. She had an enormous smile and heart for everyone she met. When I was in early elementary school, a lawyer in my parents' Bible study group in Pittsburgh introduced the idea of her working at his firm as a medical malpractice paralegal — her medical background would be an asset to the role. Mom went for it, thinking it might give her a better work-life balance, at least that was my understanding.

We moved to Texas a few years later, and she briefly returned to nursing before finding a job at a large law firm. She took me to Take Your Daughter to Work Day so I could shadow her as a medical malpractice paralegal and see how a Houston law firm functioned. I was given the task of filing paperwork in a huge room with massive filing cabinets, and I was bored out of my mind. Everyone stopped me to tell me how much they adored my mom, and that made me proud. No matter where I went — school, church, the barn, around the neighborhood, her office — people were always full of love for my mom and her kind, gentle spirit. There was, however, an incident during that day that I will never forget. The lawyer for whom she worked directly berated her in front of me. He yelled and talked down to her as if she were stupid. It was horrific, and I felt myself shrinking with her. His one-sided tirade appeared to last minutes, but it was probably 30 seconds. I was standing right next to her, and I had never heard anyone speak to my mother — or anyone else — that way. I was frightened, and I wondered how he spoke to her when I wasn't there.

A few years later, my mom joined another paralegal's company. The company consisted of Mom and the owner, and they worked from their own homes — decades before that was normal. Mom often couldn't get work done "because there's a cat in my lap." It is one of the few things I can still hear her say, and I love that memory. Law firms would outsource medical malpractice needs to this little paralegal company. The owner had previously been diagnosed with cancer and had gone through chemotherapy. Apparently, she was a great resource when Mom was diagnosed with her brain tumor — I was in England for almost that entire time, and I only know details like this when my dad has sporadically shared them over the years.

I never say that Mom had brain cancer, because no one ever used the word "cancer." There wasn't time. It was a tumor, and Mom was told that it was benign. She shared that news with me when I used a payphone to call her from England. I let out a huge sigh of relief and felt safe to regale her with tales of my trip. She said she'd be fine. I believed it. We all did.

I wondered why she needed brain surgery, which seemed rather dangerous, if it was benign — but she said it needed to be removed and chemotherapy would be the next step. That made sense to a kid whose complete medical knowledge came from NBC's *ER*. Mom told me that my brother was joking that I "gave her the tumor," because the doctors estimated it had been there for fifteen years. That would mean it appeared and started growing during my terrible twos. I didn't laugh. I knew Nate was trying to ease the situation, but I also knew I wouldn't be able to get away with that joke like he did. I would've been yelled at for it — but Mom couldn't stop laughing about Nate's joke pinning her tumor on me. It helped her cope and relaxed her, and that was a gift.

After Mom's death, our family doctor came to the house. He lived a few doors down the street, and he had helped get Mom into a big-name hospital when the tumor was found. He came bearing news we hadn't asked for and didn't want. He sat in our living room and said that he'd gone through her pathology report. Her tumor was not benign. They lied.

He said it was actually a very aggressive tumor. According to him, if she had lived, she likely would've survived 9–18 months, and those months would've been filled with harsh chemotherapy and radiation. My mom would've suffered. We would've been able to say "goodbye," but she would've suffered immensely. I don't know what scenario would've been better for us — she'd die no matter what — but her sudden death seemed, at least, better for her. People frequently ask me if sudden death or death after a long illness is worse. They're both awful. Someone we love dies regardless.

I was angry and confused. What was the point of the doctors lying to her? What was the purpose of them lying to us? Why did that neurologist put his arm around me and tell me, "She'll be riding that horse of yours in two weeks?" My distrust of providers began that day, with their false hope and lies, and it continues today.

Early in 1999, my dad shared that the owner of the medical malpractice paralegal company Mom worked for had raised the idea of us suing the hospital or the doctor — I'm not sure which. Maybe both. It must've been part of my dad's grief, but he left it up to me to decide whether we pursued legal action. Yes, a 17-year-old was asked to decide if our family would sue one of the largest hospitals in the world. I thought about all the stories Mom had told me about court — "If only he had put that in the chart," or the reverse, "If only he hadn't put that in the chart." I thought about the countless times I'd seen Sam Waterston in court on *Law & Order*, and Mom watching *L.A. Law* when I was a kid. I thought about that terrible lawyer who screamed at Mom in front of me. None of that sounded like how my last semester in high school should go. I said, "No." My reasoning was simple: I didn't want to spend my last few months at home in court. I knew no money would bring my mom back. If she couldn't come back, what was the point?

Years later, I learned the point. The point was account-ability — keeping them from doing the same thing to another family. I also didn't understand the legal system. In my mind, we'd file the lawsuit and be in court within the next few weeks. I had no idea that lawyers would likely tie that up for years. All I could imagine was sitting in a *Law & Order*-style courtroom, having to tell a jury about the last days of my mom's life rather than facing my grief. I didn't like that image. I knew very little about the medical and legal systems except what TV told me. I made the decision a grieving 17-year-old could make, but I wouldn't make the same choice today.

Even now, decades later, I am still hesitant to trust doctors for my own care. I trust the ones I work alongside — I can ask them questions, watch them interact with staff, patients, and families, listen to how they think, read their chart notes. Perhaps I should see a veterinarian for my regular care, like Kramer did when he had a cough. I have enormous trust in the veterinarians who care for my dogs and horse. I continue to have frequent headaches, and friends often ask what the root cause is when I tell them how often they occur. I don't know. People regularly encourage me to "get those headaches checked out." I refuse. Why would I? In my mind, only one result is possible: they'll find a tumor. I don't trust I'll get proper care if there is one. Every time I get a headache, I pop some Excedrin Migraine, get a bit anxious, and think, "it's either a tumor or nothing." And I go about my day hoping the medication works, slightly concerned about how much I rely on those over-the-counter pills. I doubt I will ever follow through on an MRI to learn more about my headaches. They lied about my mom's, and she's dead. I don't need to be lied to and learn about a tumor, too. I'd rather enjoy each day without wondering if I can trust any diagnostics regarding my headaches or any other ailments.

My distrust of providers began with my mom's last 11 days of life, and working in healthcare seemed to give me permission to avoid doctor visits for myself. Whenever I make an appointment, it's almost alarming to those closest to me. Like many healthcare workers, I'm one of the last to make a doctor's appointment when something ails me. I push through it, lean on clinical knowledge gained through chart review and countless conversations with providers, get advice from colleagues, or I simply ignore it. That has been my norm for a long time, and this year is giving me every excuse to put off my own care.

In 2009, I underwent laparoscopic surgery to discover if I had endometriosis. This came after months of ruling out every other possible diagnosis that could explain my debilitating pain. I remember being in the fetal position at 2 a.m., screaming in pain as I held my hands over my abdomen. There were times, while walking the dogs, when I had to sit on the side of a busy road and wait for the pain to pass. The surgery proved to be successful, if we want to call it that. Doctors and endometriosis sufferers will all tell you that the dreaded disease returns. There is no complete cure, nor much research on endometriosis.

The day my endometriosis came back was pretty clear. I suddenly had excruciating pain and knew right away what it was. At times, I felt like an endometriosis impostor, because I didn't have multiple surgeries like countless other women. My pain was also relatively tolerable. In hindsight, I realized that my pain was neither normal nor tolerable. I simply pushed through it, because I didn't want to tell a doctor. In 2025, however, I started having new symptoms — regular morning vomiting, pain in new places that wouldn't let up. I went to my PCP and had all sorts of tests done. They wondered if it was a gastrointestinal issue, and I remembered that my first ovarian cyst at age 11 was originally diagnosed as appendicitis. The PCP office did some bloodwork, ordered a CT that I never got out of stubbornness, and referred me to a new OB-GYN.

My fiancé, Patrick, wanted me to have answers before I left for a trip to Ireland, because he was worried something could happen while abroad. He is constantly ready to protect me and advocate for me, and those qualities give me peace after years of feeling abandoned. Even his concern that I could have a medical issue while abroad was heartening. I reasoned, however, that I didn't want any news to halt my trip — and if there was an issue while I was in Ireland or the UK, I could take advantage of their free healthcare. I packed a ton of ibuprofen on the trip like a good middle-aged equestrian with chronic pain. The physician's assistant at the OB-GYN's office did not hide her concern when she heard my personal history, family history, and symptoms. Her hackles went up during the physical exam; I reported my "constant pain is a 4 out of 5 and goes up from there," and more tests were ordered in what was intended to be a simple annual checkup. I returned a couple of weeks later for a vaginal ultrasound that revealed four or five cysts of significant size. The endometriosis wasn't just back. It was severe — the endometriomas were large enough for her to repeatedly caution me about ovarian torsion, and she raised the idea of a hysterectomy. We discussed my remaining, if complicated, hopes of becoming a mother, and how stage IV endometriosis, as well as age, could impact that. I was scheduled to speak with the obstetrician about surgery in a couple of weeks. The day before the appointment, I canceled it.

There are three reasons why I canceled the appointment. First, our healthcare system needs some major adjustments. I didn't want to be told that surgery was necessary and needed to be done soon, because then I'd fulfill my deductible too late in the year to use it well. I'd prefer to have the surgery in the first quarter of 2026 — assuming the grief math let me live longer than my mom — giving me a full year to see any specialist I wanted without more money draining from my pocket. Second, any endometriosis warrior will encourage you to have your surgery done by an excision specialist. Not every gynecologist is fully trained to remove endometriosis, and we'd all like to limit how often we return to the OR. Having a conversation about surgery with someone I wouldn't let take me under the knife would've been futile. My OB-GYN may be good, but he isn't an excision specialist. I found a local specialist and knew he'd be who I'd see if the pain became intolerable — I aimed to put off requesting an appointment with him for the same insurance reason.

The third and final reason I canceled the appointment comes back to grief math. Since doctors lied about my mom's tumor in 1998, I've been hesitant to see doctors and to trust them unless they work in pediatrics. In 2019, a horse fall led to breaking two metacarpals in my right hand and three transverse process fractures in my left lumbar. There was nothing to be done for my lumbar except pain medications and time. An orthopedic surgeon suggested surgery for my hand to insert screws. I hated the idea of going under anesthesia, and I sought counsel from the Chief Surgical Officer at the hospital where I was serving as a chaplain. He was a pediatric orthopedic surgeon, and he agreed that surgery was a better option than a cast with an unknown outcome. I had the surgery and was apparently asking for prayer bubbles — one of my favorite interventions for helping kids process anxiety. I went through with it because it was necessary. It wasn't completely elective. If I underwent a hysterectomy, it might be recommended, but would still qualify as elective at this point. I wouldn't want to do that any year, let alone this one. This is, after all, the year grief math tells me I will die, and I can't put the odds of that being true in the hands of a doctor and an operating table.

My mom died in the OR after collapsing in her hospital bed two days after neurosurgery. Her provider said she had congestive heart failure, but I don't believe a thing he said. He also said her tumor was benign, and she'd be riding Dancer again in two weeks. Regardless, I am now her age. The grief math is mathing. I canceled my OB-GYN appointment because I refuse to have elective surgery at the same age my mother was when she died — and because I still question the decisions of physicians who don't work in pediatrics, thanks to her doctor. I'll take all the over-the-counter pain medications available, press heating pads on my abdomen, practice deep breathing, and wince through the pain, but I will not go under general anesthesia and be wheeled into an OR at age 44. It seems irresponsible to agree to surgery from where I stand — a young griever watching the final grief math problems approach. I hesitate to trust new providers, procedures that don't guarantee healing, and the grief math. There is so much trauma still rooted in one doctor telling a lie, wrapping his arm around me, and offering me hope that my horse-loving mom would be riding again soon — while he already knew her tumor was aggressive and would end her life. Those lies were far from sweet, and they've shaped me for 27 years.

———

VIII

The First Year

MY BROTHER'S 21ST BIRTHDAY was six days after Mom died, and Christmas was a week after that. That first Christmas is a blur. I remember coming downstairs the first couple of mornings after she died. I would wake up, forget she was dead, and then see every flat surface covered in flowers. One day, all the flowers wilted and died, too.

On New Year's Eve, I went to a party, thinking that was a good idea. As 1999 approached, the host blared Prince's "Party Like It's 1999." I was numb. I remember standing frozen in the middle of someone's living room and staring at the clock on their VCR. "She won't see this year," I thought. She'd been gone only two weeks, and she was already missing a new year. I felt like the only person there — maybe the only person for miles — but there were dozens of drunk teenagers filling that house. I don't remember anyone speaking to me, but given how thoughtfully they cared for me at school, they were likely checking on me every few minutes with little to no response from me. I just stared at that VCR as if I were looking right into 1999, the first of infinite years Mom would never experience and that I would have to survive without her. My grief math was beginning to expand beyond those first twelve days of December 1998, as each month, holiday, and milestone I passed without her started adding up.

The last semester of high school should be full of excitement and anticipation for the future and independence. Most 18-year-olds are finalizing college applications and planning senior pranks and parties. I did those things — strolling around my little school, going through the motions of a senior — while being in a daze, numb, or randomly bursting into tears.

Children often engage in rebellious or regressive behavior when they're grieving. For example, kids who haven't had a potty accident in years may start wetting the bed again, and straight-A students without a single detention to their name may start making Cs or skipping class. I did exactly what my mom had been telling me to: drink alcohol. Up until Mom's death, I went to every alcohol-filled high school party and stayed sober. It was well-known that no one could convince me to drink, and there was always a six-pack of Coke in the fridge for me at whoever's house we were terrorizing. I took care of vomiting 16-year-olds and even remember cops breaking up a party while a freshman vomited in my lap while I held back her hair. My mom was aware of what was happening at these parties, as were most of the parents. My friends' parents didn't care because they were European and found the drinking age to be too high in the United States anyway. My mom kept telling me to have a beer at the parties. "Moderation is fine. Live a little," she'd say to me. I couldn't believe it, and I'd tell her how crazy it was that she was pushing me to drink. "I'm just worried you're being too stiff. I want people to like you." The first party after her death, I immediately grabbed a rum and Coke from the hostess. No one said a word. From then on, I was trashed at those high school parties. Years later, I wondered why no one stopped me and said, "Hey. You're obviously only drinking because you're sad. You never drank before." I think they were happy I was finally joining in — but without a single sober person at the parties, we lost the ability to make the 2 a.m. drives to Whataburger for taquitos that I regularly did to fulfill late-night cravings and get food in everyone's stomachs. We were all smart enough not to drive and slept spread out all over the main hostess's house. In my grief, I rebelled in the exact way my mom had been pressuring me to, and there's a bit of humor in that — except I don't think she intended for my drinking bad beer and poorly mixed cocktails to inevitably lead to me sobbing loudly about her death in a sea of drunk teenagers.

I am grateful to have had my barn family and the community at my tight-knit international school. The people at both places — and the horses at the former — made me feel safe. My school stopped counting absences, allowing me to come in late or leave if grief was smacking me in the face a bit extra that day. Classmates and teachers surrounded me with such love and grace, despite not knowing what to say or do. I vividly remember sobbing in my car in the student parking lot, only to find my best friend standing outside my car. He was in class, and someone had spotted me crying. They ran to his classroom, and his teacher didn't hesitate to let him leave to be with me. On the twelfth of every month, I would shatter. I'd cry intermittently through the day, and I felt safe to cry openly at school. I never felt judged or pressured to cope a certain way. It was as if each full month without her was like that first night in December. The twelfth of each month was a monthly grief math equation. I could feel her fading from me with every new month without her.

The barn was safe, too. People there knew my mom, and they had witnessed her at her happiest. Each of them had been part of giving my mom her dream of riding and owning her own horse. The teenagers saw her as one of the loving barn moms. Her fellow amateur riders saw her as a peer. Our horse was easily the tallest at the barn. When she rode him, she'd yell, "Do I look like a pea on him?" I'd say she didn't, and it made me laugh that being on a big horse was the only time she really seemed self-conscious about her height. We're both under five feet. Being at school or the barn kept me going. Home was hard. It felt empty, and my dad still traveled quite a bit for work. There was some joy that year. Dancer was able to show for the first time after a year off for hock surgery, and it had been unclear whether that could happen again. It was bittersweet to glide with him over jumps in the show ring without her there — heavy and freeing all at once. Every time I rode him, I felt her with me.

I was regularly told by adults to "be strong for your dad." To be honest, I'm relieved that my mom didn't die earlier, for reasons that may surprise people. If I had been younger, I think I would've been guilted into staying in Houston to take care of my dad. That's what I was told to do — but I had made up my mind to leave Texas for college when we moved there in 1991. It is all too common that young girls are told to give up their dreams to care for their family, yet it was shocking that people were still suggesting it in 1998. The pressure from adults to care for him made me hold back from telling him that I needed grief support myself. Houston has a well-known nonprofit for grieving children, and I wanted to go. There was something on their website about parents having a support group while the kids were in one, and I was somehow under the impression that parents had to attend rather than that being an option. Because of that, I never went. I didn't want my dad to think I needed help, and he never asked if I did. Shame was rampant because of people's comments and instructions that I needed to "be strong for my dad." Guilt and shame are common in grief — something I know now but was unaware of at 17. I was supposed to help him grieve, and that didn't seem possible if he knew how much I was hurting. Even as a teenager, I thought, "That's pretty harsh to say to an impressionable young person." Thank goodness I didn't listen, but it made me feel terribly guilty for leaving for college. A lot of things in life aren't fair, but making a grieving teen girl feel guilty for not turning her already upsetting life upside down to care for her dad — who was, after all, a middle-aged adult — is awful. I still wonder why those adults didn't choose to support my dad rather than push me to do it. I needed adults, including my dad, to be honest, patient, and com-passionate — present for me in my grief. Those are charac-teristics all children and adolescents, including me, need for healthy coping in grief. I needed examples of how to move through it and people to love me like only a mom could.

While my college choice was certainly shaped by my mom's death, I still stayed true to my goal of leaving Texas. My fear was that people's instructions to be my dad's caregiver would've minimized my own opportunities. I planned to go to American University or Boston University to study international affairs or something similar. I had no idea what that major entailed, but my love for other cultures led me there. Mom agreed that I needed to go to a big school after graduating from a high school with a senior class size of 48, including the French section. On our college tour, we looked at small women's liberal arts colleges, too, because of their riding programs. Given that I now had to fulfill Mom's promise to keep Dancer safe for the rest of his life, I changed my plans. I was accepted everywhere I applied. American University gave me a minimal scholarship, but I couldn't figure out how to juggle riding in Washington, D.C., especially when freshmen couldn't have a car. Dancer needed to be close — for him, for Mom, and for me. Sweet Briar College gave me a nearly full academic scholarship, and he was accepted for the time being, too. Enrolling at a small women's college was exactly what I needed after losing the main female guide in my life.

No matter where I was, I felt numb that first year. It felt as though everyone knew but also no one knew. Leaving for college was good for me, although it was hard to navigate friendships when you were Dead Mom Girl, still adjusting to that new normal every day.

Bereaved adolescents experience strong feelings of abandonment. We wonder why our parent left, even when they didn't have a choice. She died. She left me. I was abandoned, and I needed her.

This all-too-normal feeling of abandonment was deeply projected onto friendships, but I was not aware of what was happening. In college, I would see my friends walk right by my dorm room to head to the cafeteria to eat together. Did they purposely not invite me? Was it an oversight? Either way, being left out for something normal — something we all did — hit as hard as a breakup every single time. I would develop incredibly deep friendships quickly, but then my grief would become an issue. Some would have more grace than others. Because I didn't always recognize my emotional responses to female dynamics as grief, there was no way that they could. I would interpret any action or statement from them as rejection, and I would become attached or pull away from something that someone who wasn't freshly bereaved would be able to ignore. Sometimes they meant to hurt or forget me. Sometimes they weren't aware of what they were doing. My grief doesn't excuse all my friends' behavior, but it does often explain my reaction to it — particularly when my reaction didn't seem to match the action.

My freshman roommate moved out, and I never knew why. I wouldn't be surprised if being around a girl in raw grief was too much. I was a bit unpredictable, and there are so many things I now look back on and say, "Oh, that was the grief talking." The horse girls stopped hanging around me when I stopped riding at the college riding center. Strong friendships were built, then fizzled. Each time, I felt abandoned. That sense of abandonment hit just as hard when my whole friend group went to the nearby men's college for parties without me as it did when a close friendship suddenly ended. Years later, I understood what was happening. If only I could have articulated it then. Some would have understood. Some would have shown their true colors. Regardless, I would know who my friends truly were. Feelings of abandonment were heightened the first year after my mom's death and continued for years afterward. The feeling lessened with self-awareness but never went away.

Every holiday and birthday was met with fear and heavy emotions that first year. Even minor holidays, such as St. Patrick's Day, had a memory attached to them, because my mom loved to celebrate the tiniest moments. Leprechauns hid presents in our house when we were kids, and she left us Valentine's Day gifts. The twelfth of every month, major and minor holidays, my mom's birthday, my birthday, Easter, Thanksgiving, and Christmas were filled with tears as memories hit like a horse's hoof to the stomach. It seemed it was up to me to maintain any family traditions, and I did the best I could.

My mom filled the house with joy. We argued, for sure, but she knew how to make the most mundane moment special. Despite her magic, she still couldn't make pulling the weeds in the garden enjoyable for me — but she put her touch onto everything. Because of this, her absence was palpable. I'm not sure I realized how much she actually did for us until she wasn't there to do it. Major and minor holidays, as well as accomplishments of all sizes, were a reminder of her gentle way of showing her family, neighbors, coworkers, and barn mates that they were loved. It didn't take long before that became a part of my personality, too.

IX

Annual "Mom Day"

GRIEF MATH BRINGS NEW ANSWERS every December 12. The anniversary of her death arrives, and a couple of months later my birthday follows — each one drawing me closer to the age she was when she died. On the anniversary, all I need to do is subtract 1998 from the current year, and I am reminded of how long she's been gone. December 12 is the last day she lived, and, like many grievers, that day looms on the calendar. I'm not sure why it isn't an automatic holiday on all Apple products. Since the first anniversary, I have been very intentional about how that day is spent. Giving the day energy and attention — what I often call "Mom Day" — allows me to celebrate her life and mark a significant date on the grief math calendar. It's something I can control.

Anytime I talk to someone approaching the death anniversary of a loved one, whether in a professional or personal context, they describe how the days leading up to it are full of fear, anxiety, and uncertainty. We wonder how we will feel on that day. There's a deep sense of dread. Each year, I wish we could simply skip over the 12th and move right on to December 13. December 13 always feels like a fresh start — proof that there's no turning back, and proof that I made it through another year. Grief math causes me to read that last sentence in two different ways. Positive: I made it through another year. I survived without a mother's guidance, advice, comfort, and love. Negative: I lived yet another year without my mom, and she is still gone.

In my professional life, people often ask for guidance on how to handle a death anniversary. Families never know that many of my ideas are rooted in my personal life as much as in professional experience, and they don't need to know. A good chaplain, therapist, or counselor doesn't disclose their own story — rather, they use it quietly to inform their care. I acknowledge the complex emotions as the day approaches and ask minimally guided questions to help people discover what will make the day meaningful for them.

I've become practiced at shaping a death anniversary into a day of healing — for the people I care for and for myself.

The first anniversary of my mom's death fell near the end of my first semester of college. I'm lucky that Sweet Briar College had self-scheduled final exams. The 12th often landed within the exam week, and I'd simply not schedule any that day. For that first year, I decided I would do things that Mom did when she was sad, stressed, or upset in any way. My friends were focused on exams, but they didn't want to leave me to face the day alone. They divided up the activities so that someone was always with me and no one would lose study time. One friend went shopping with me, others went out to eat, and another offered to go on a trail ride through Sweet Briar's extensive riding trails. Unfortunately, my horse was incredibly fresh from the colder weather, and I ended up going back to the barn to lunge him while the others continued without me. I imagine he could feel my heightened emotions that day — and I know he grieved my mom, too. Right after she died, he repeatedly jumped out of the pasture, something he had never done before. The barn's groom told me, "Your mom is jumping him from Heaven." He grieved, and it was hard that he couldn't settle enough on that first anniversary for a therapeutic trail ride. It made sense, though.

During that week, my college riding trainer asked to meet with me in the evening. She told me my horse wasn't welcome at the school anymore. He "didn't fit the program." We had just a few days before the winter holiday would shut down the school for a month. Sweet Briar isn't a massive state university that always has something happening. During school breaks, you can't be in the dorms. The campus is deserted. Our lovely women's college in the Blue Ridge Mountains goes quiet. How was I supposed to find a new home for my horse in Virginia while taking exams and dealing with the first anniversary of my mother's death, leave him there, then go home to Texas for a month? I decided to send him home to Texas, and I never rode at Sweet Briar again — despite the riding program being what had drawn me there. The trainer said she wanted me to keep riding there, and the Director of Riding said the same the following semester, when I took a Sporting Horses course he co-taught with an art history professor. In my mind, if you didn't accept my horse, you didn't accept me. The thing is, this was grief.

My horse was the only thing that connected me to Mom, and they wanted to separate us. He was the only thing that kept me happy, healthy, and in a good routine my first semester of college. He had some trouble adjusting to rural Virginia from bustling Houston, and the college didn't have patience for that. I do believe that if I were a rider in a different tax bracket, that conversation never would've happened. He would've been welcomed, and I would've felt more encouraged as a rider rather than judged. Such is the life of an equestrian who doesn't have generational wealth. There could not have been a worse week to be told that my horse was getting kicked out of college — and the reasoning was vague. It was a gut punch. I was surviving grief because he was with me. I vividly remember sobbing in a dark area where chairs and tables were stored, between the cafeteria and the back staircase that led to my dorm. Either my roommate or the girls who lived across the hall found me on their way to or from dinner. The one thing that made me feel as though I belonged at that school and still close to my mom was being taken from me. I was shattered.

That first year set a precedent for how each December 12 would be spent, and it was striking to watch how it evolved. The first few years, I was very intentional about doing things Mom loved, even if I didn't. Over time, as I grew into adulthood, those same activities became things I genuinely loved and felt emotionally and physically safe doing. A good example is hiking. Growing up, anytime there was a day off school, Mom made us go hiking. Once Nate was older, he didn't have to come, but I always did. I hated it. Years later, when I had my own dogs, hiking became one of my favorite things — for exercise, to bond with my dogs, and to feel God's presence.

December 12, 2001, I was living in France as part of a study abroad program. My friends and I gathered at an

Irish pub in the fifth arrondissement to toast my mom. She would've loved the idea of walking from the Seine, down an alleyway, and into a warm pub decorated for Christmas.

In seminary, I would spend the day alone, hiking through Austin's many parks and greenbelts. In the evening, friends would join me for dinner. That tradition continued after school, and I replaced Austin's outdoor spaces with the Houston Arboretum. Mom adored the Houston Arboretum. For many years, I would take my dog — and later, as the pack grew, more dogs — through the Arboretum as part of my December 12 ritual.

On the 10th anniversary of Mom's death, I was living in Pennsylvania serving as a pediatric chaplain. It was the closest I'd been to the cemetery since we buried her ashes — about a four-hour drive across the state. Oliver, my soul dog, made the drive with me in the snow. I arrived at Sewickley Cemetery and searched for the plots belonging to my dad's side of the family. I found my mom near my beloved Beebaw and Papa, my dad's parents. She was so loved by them. I brushed the snow off all their headstones and cried. I felt so alone while I stared at their resting places. After a while, Oliver and I drove back the way we came. I have never been back to the graveside again. Sometimes I wish Americans respected and honored cemeteries the way Europeans — especially the French — do. It seems as though we are taught to fear cemeteries when we're kids. In France, people go on reflective, daily walks in cemeteries or have their lunch on a bench near a famous author's grave. In the United States, visiting a cemetery is almost considered morbid. I hope people feel more comfortable taking care of graves and visiting their loved ones if it helps them. Being so far from Mom's grave doesn't bother me — but I do wish our culture was more open about it, and less intent on teaching kids to hold their breath as they drive by one out of superstition.

Back in Houston, I always took December 12 off work. If I had an office job, I don't know if I would still do that — but I provide spiritual and emotional support to people dealing with cancer, trauma, and end-of-life situations both before and after death. I don't think I would be the chaplain they need on that day, and it wouldn't be kind to the patients, families, or hospital staff. It wouldn't be kind to me. One year, I had to take a half day because the other chaplain couldn't cover the weekly hospital chapel service that happened to land on the 12th. In those few hours at work, I helped an 11-year-old cancer patient and his mom understand his cancer had spread and there were no more options. He was a very special boy whose last words to me were, "You're family." It was too much on that day. I got a ticket on the way home for not fully stopping at a stop sign and spent the rest of the day with the dogs until dinner. From then on, I was adamant about taking that day off.

Until I moved to Houston's suburbs, the Houston Arboretum was part of the day. Every year, we would eat dinner at my mom's favorite restaurant, The Black Lab, and my fiancé would give a remarkable toast to my mom that would make you think he knew her well — yet we met more than a decade after she died. He listens to stories, asks questions, and is probably able to see how I take after my mom better than I do, just from the memories I've shared.

My mom loved The Black Lab, and she went a few times with friends and took me there after visiting the Museum of Fine Arts. It was an authentic British pub in Houston's Montrose neighborhood. The floors were heavy wood, the tables and booths made from similar material. At Christmas, the greenery was fresh and fragrant and transported you to the

Cotswolds. It was the perfect place to celebrate my mom's life. Once I moved to the suburbs, the almost-hour drive to The Black Lab seemed crazy, but we kept doing it. As I approached 21 years after she died, I said, "Maybe it's time we find somewhere closer that she would've liked." Oddly, a day or so later, I saw a post on social media that The Black Lab was closing after 33 years. My high school Spanish teacher saw my Facebook post lamenting the impending closure and encouraged me to see if I could purchase some memorabilia from the restaurant. I called ahead and talked to the staff. After explaining why I eat there every December 12, they told me to ask to speak to the manager when we came for dinner.

The manager met me at our table and asked to hear directly from me why The Black Lab was so special to my mom and, now, to me. He asked to hear stories about my mom, and I was taken aback by that. It had been a long time since anyone had asked me such a thoughtful question — and he was a stranger. He listened intently. After we ate, he told me to walk around the restaurant and pick a piece of artwork I liked. I found a painting of an English hunt riding scene. I knew right away that it was the one, because both my mom and I would've purchased it on our own. I asked him how much, and I was prepared to spend an amount I'd probably regret in the morning. He simply said he'd take it down and meet me outside. He said, "Exit out front the way you normally would, then go to the side of the pub." Standing on a dark sidewalk with large oak trees overhead, he handed me two T-shirts with the pub's logo and the painting. He wouldn't let me pay. That lovely piece of art now hangs above my mom's saddle in my home. Three days later, The Black Lab closed, and I felt Mom slipping further away as one more place she knew and loved was gone.

The years that I had access to a horse always made me feel closer to Mom. Nothing made her happier than horse time, and that's something we share. On my way to the barn each December 12, I hope that no one else is there. I want it to be only Gunner and me, and I tell him that Grandma Bee is with us. It's not that I don't want to see other people — it's just that it's the one day of the year I don't have the energy for small talk, and I want to keep the day as sacred as possible. I do often let one or two trusted barn mates or my trainer know what the day is, in case they wonder why I'm quieter than usual or tear up without warning. There are few places left that are as sacred as a barn for a horse girl, especially a horse girl who is the daughter of a horse girl.

Each year, I make a social media post about Mom on December 12. I make that post later in the day every year, because I feel some shame about it. I wonder if people notice it and think, "Isn't she over that yet?" And they might. But there is no timeline on grief. If I like to celebrate who she was by making a reel of photos of her set to songs such as Taylor Swift's "Marjorie," then who does that hurt? They can keep scrolling. Finding the photos, scanning them, and making the post allows me to cry and try to remember her. It's another way to say, "I love you, and I miss you."

The anniversary of a loved one's death doesn't have to be just any other day. It can be painful. It can be joyful. It can be both. In my personal and professional lives, I hear a lot about what the death anniversary can mean to people. I am open and vulnerable about how fiercely and intentionally I face the day, and I hope my way of honoring Mom Day gives others permission to do the same. My rituals give me control as the grief math reminds me how long she has been gone. I fill Mom Day with dogs, horses, and nature, and the day ends with a dinner in her honor. Most years, I browse old photographs and go through a box of cards and notes — sent in the weeks following her death, or gathered later as part of a project where I wrote to her friends and family. The cards, letters, and photographs bring her to life for me. They may bring heavy tears, but those moments are tender, and I feel connected to her. That's the point of Mom Day, really. It's a celebration of her life and a way to feel close to her — and one of the ways I tell her that I still love her.

Lifetime Club Membership

TWO WEEKS AFTER MY MOTHER'S DEATH, our neighborhood swim team's former assistant coach rang our doorbell. Her mom had died when she was 12. She lived a few blocks away and was a year or two older than my brother. There were six kids in their family, and their house was the "cool house." I was surprised to see her at my door — she had long since gone off to college. She handed me a plastic bag and told me to "open this when you're ready."

Predictably, I waited about 30 seconds once I was alone in my bedroom to open the bag. It was a book, and the title was the name of a club I had not asked to join. It was called *Motherless Daughters* and was written by Hope Edelman. In middle school, I joined a French Club with an embarrassing amount of enthusiasm. In college, I was "tapped" into a club for loud and silly girls. In seminary, I joined and co-led a club based on the verse Acts 2:42. But this club? Nope. I didn't sign my name on a clipboard. It wasn't a choice. My membership was solidified for the rest of my life, though, and there was no way to decline or resign. I am a Motherless Daughter.

The book quickly became a treasured one. It was carefully stuffed in carry-on luggage with my Bible — to Europe, to visit grandparents, to college. It went everywhere with me. Some chapters were read repeatedly, and some have yet to be read. *Motherless Daughters* is a heavy name. There are countless women with membership to the club, and few want it. Twenty-seven years after her death, I have recommended that book to dozens of women in my life, some of whom I know well and some I barely know at all. Recently, I was on a bereavement call with a woman in her 60s. Her mother died seven months prior, at just shy of 100 years old. Most adult children her age tell me they're "at peace" after their elderly parents' death and elaborate on why. This woman, however, has heavy, therapeutic cries every time I call to check in and remind her that support is available. On this particular call, I told her about the *Motherless Daugh-*

ters book. "The author interviewed women who lost their mothers at all different ages, especially children and teenagers," I explained. "Oh, goodness!" she interrupted. "I can't handle my mom's death, and she lived into her late 90s. Can you imagine losing your mom as a kid or a teenager?" "Awful. Such a nightmare," I said, fighting tears on the other end of the phone. Yes, yes, I can imagine. She would never know that I was in the same club — that even as I validated her tears, her pain, her grief, her point of view, I was doing so without revealing my own history. She would never know that I've been a club member since I was a teenager.

When someone we love dies, there are two parts of us. There is who we were when they were alive, and who we are after they died. We are never the same. I have no idea what my profession would be or where I'd live if my mom were still alive. I am certain that dogs and horses would still be in my life in a central way, and we would share our passion for horses even more than we did when I was a teenager.

Being a Motherless Daughter is part of my identity. When I used to care for childhood cancer patients in their teens, I regularly asked them to share three or more things about themselves that make them who they are but have nothing to do with cancer. If I chaplained myself and asked for three or more things that define me, I would tell people within the hospital walls that dogs, horses, and Arsenal are a massive part of who I am — as well as my faith. You'd think faith would be obvious, but I've seen so many chaplains struggle with their faith after seeing the things we see when climbing into the mess with others. When I'm outside of work with people who truly know my heart, I will add a profound part of my identity that the casual person does not need to know (mostly because of the tilted head and odd "I'm sorry" response). I am a Motherless Daughter. While I wish I weren't a part of the club with a lifetime membership, I am proud of my resilience, my ability to face grief, and my capacity to navigate the biggest and smallest parts of life without a mother by my side.

XI

Mother's Day is the Worst

THE FIRST MOTHER'S DAY was painful, and now it's mostly irritating — a cloud of emptiness and sadness hanging over it. Every year, however, I say to myself, "Maybe next year I'll have my own kid, and Mother's Day will take on new meaning." It seems this is the one holiday that has yet to be reframed, as every year the grief compounds: I remain both motherless and childless on Mother's Day. That first one set the tone for every one that followed.

Mother's Day 1999 was the annual day in my church when graduating high school seniors would stand on the chancel — the raised area at the front of a traditional sanctuary — and announce where they would be attending college. Each student's parents would stand up in their pew as their child's name was called. Not only was it my first Mother's Day as a motherless daughter, but it was also the first time I had only one parent representing me in such a public way.

I stood in a line of 17- and 18-year-old high school seniors and faced our giant Presbyterian congregation in west Houston. I felt physically ill looking out at the sea of mothers holding flowers, parents beaming, and a congregation thrilled to see kids they had taught in Sunday school and led on mission trips preparing for the next step in their lives. "Jessica Shannon, Sweet Briar College," called out the youth leader. My dad rose from his seat. He looked so lonely in that massive sanctuary as he stood by himself. I hated that we were both experiencing this moment and so far from each other, making it impossible for a hug. There was no other kid on the chancel with a solo parent standing in the crowd. The foreshadowing was strong that day.

Sadness over Mother's Day began well before the actual day, as commercials popped up with gift ideas to celebrate the moms in our lives. I hated each commercial. Avoiding the card aisle at CVS is often a goal, but somehow I always ended up in the wrong aisle while trying to find the cruelty-free shampoo. It's a difficult holiday to hide from, but I've discovered a few ways to protect myself. Unfortunately, there were painful lessons to learn along the way. It was soon clear that stores weren't the only ones pushing this holiday. Restaurants advertised brunch specials. As online shopping became the norm, every store I ever ordered from would send Mother's Day emails with links to items they thought our moms would like. I wonder how much money I've saved in the last 27 years without buying Mom a new riding shirt, framed picture, or jewelry she probably would not have worn. A few years ago, Draper James — a classic clothing store owned by Reese Witherspoon — sent out an email a few weeks before Mother's Day that forever made me a fan of the brand. The email acknowledged that the upcoming holiday is hard for many women: whether their relationship with their mother was strained, their mother is deceased, or they have struggled with infertility and miscarriage. The email gave Draper James customers the option to opt out of any Mother's Day emails. I clicked "opt out" as quickly as possible and let my fellow motherless daughters know about the thoughtfulness of that Southern clothing store.

For weeks leading up to the day itself, there are constant reminders to motherless daughters that a hard day is on the horizon. We can't avoid the commercials, emails, and social media ads. We can make that a Sunday where we skip brunch — and that's not the only thing I skip that Sunday. It is the one day of the year I refuse to attend church.

There have been a few Mother's Days where church was unavoidable. One was my first Mother's Day without her. Years later, I was on staff at a church, and Sunday was a workday. I learned then that, after Christmas Eve and Easter, Mother's Day is the highest-attended church service of the calendar year, and Father's Day is the lowest. Other than that, I tried not to attend church on Mother's Day. When I did, it was a rude reminder of why it was painful.

Many churches hand every woman over a certain age a flower and wish them "Happy Mother's Day!" They assume each woman in her mid-20s and older is a mother. What they are not considering is that any one of those women could be struggling to become a mother, missing her own mother, or both. Once, I tried entering the sanctuary from a side door, and a greeter still trapped me. That was my last attempt to worship on Mother's Day.

Twenty-seven years later, I don't go anywhere except the barn on that holiday. I want all my friends who are moms to enjoy being celebrated while honoring their own moms — but at my age, every cashier at the grocery store, waiter at a restaurant, and church volunteer or staff member happily wishes me a "Happy Mother's Day." It is anything but happy. I can keep it lukewarm if I focus on an Arsenal match, dogs, and my horse. Mother's Day has become the one day of the year where I try to avoid everyone who doesn't have four legs. Those innocent wishes for a happy day cut more and more with each greeting. I've learned it's best to steer clear of everyone. It keeps the day from being awkward for friends who are aware I'm a motherless daughter, and protects me from being bombarded by strangers and casual acquaintances. While I don't condone avoidance as a coping strategy, it's actually safe and healthy on this one holiday. Every Mother's Day, grief math adds another year and another holiday she missed. It's a harsh day — and for my own sake, I avoid it as best I can. Sometimes, avoidance is exactly what is needed.

<hr>

XII

Let's Talk About Death

I WAS SO LOST AFTER Mom died. I didn't understand what was normal and what wasn't. I didn't know how to feel or what to do. There wasn't a *What to Expect When Your Mom Dies* that laid out each step the way books for expecting parents do. On nights when my emotions were particularly heavy, I would drive to a Barnes & Noble and cry in the grief and self-help sections. All alone, I pored through books and looked for answers. I thought I wanted to find validation of my feelings and a map for facing each day, but I was really looking for my mother.

I've learned that grief doesn't have a timeline, and Elizabeth Kübler-Ross's stages of grief are not a checklist. The stages were originally written for the person dying, not the bereaved — but we changed both their purpose and their intended recipient. If adults are confused and think they should be past a certain stage by a certain time, then a 17-year-old reading grief books through tears would certainly be lost navigating her new normal.

We will all lose people we love. We will all grieve. We will all die. We will all have someone grieve us. We aren't immune to death or grief. So why are we so hesitant to talk about it? Why are people so uncomfortable with the one event that everyone — regardless of socioeconomic status, race, gender, nationality, and religion — will experience? Every time someone asks me questions about my mom or my dogs, they're telling me they care. They're giving me permission to grieve. They're telling me it's safe to process the big emotions of grief, from anger to sadness. I vividly remember reading grief books in the early months of my loss that named a culture-wide silence around death, and I recognized it was true. No one really talked about it in my house, in my church except for Good Friday, or at school apart from in literature. At that time, death in movies was almost exclusively violent, and people were rarely depicted grieving in movies or on TV. I'm thankful that we now get to see characters exploring grief on shows like *This Is Us, Shrink-*

ing, Call the Midwife, and *The Pitt.* Speaking of *This Is Us* — that was almost too relatable while also healing something in me. I'm the same age as "The Big Three"; they were also 17 when their dad died, and I spent the first ten years of my life in Pittsburgh. Mom is also buried there. It would've been very healing for me as a lonely, sad 17-year-old to witness someone vulnerably processing grief on screen, and I love seeing it now. Normalizing grief makes us feel that we aren't alone.

It amazed me in 1998 and 1999 that my high school classmates talked about death better than any adults. They had no problem asking me how I was doing and genuinely wanted to know. They were honest when they said, "I don't know what to say or do, but I'm here." And they were. They were there. They asked questions, gave me grief books, and sat with me in empathy. Adults didn't know what to say or do, but they filled the air between us with platitudes and saddled me with the responsibility of keeping my dad alive, literally and figuratively. Still, no one truly guided me. The only person who would've been honest with me about death and grief was the person I was grieving.

There is no doubt in my mind that Mom would've companioned me through grief with grace, listening, vulnerability, and bravery. She may not have been the first person to whom I went for advice at the time, but she would not have let me hurt alone. She would not have let me navigate this terrible, wonderful thing called "grief" by doing my own research in books and on the internet, which was still in its infancy (we were still typing "www." before every URL). She would never have let me grieve in fear, uncertainty, and loneliness.

My mom would've grabbed a dog leash, told me to join her, and talked and listened. She also would've hand-grazed our horse, Dancer, leaned against the fence, and told me all the things I ended up needing to figure out on my own. I can picture that one. I have a fuzzy photograph of her with one foot on the fence, leaning back, holding onto Dancer's lead rope and shielding her eyes from the sun while she looked off at something. I always wish that photo were better quality, because it captures her and brings me such peace. Whatever mother-daughter drama we had, she was always honest and on my team. The irony that the only adult who wouldn't abandon me in grief is the one who I was, and am, grieving is not lost on me. We always need our mothers.

XIII

We Become What We Needed

MY BAGGAGE AS A GRIEVER is too heavy to avoid baggage fees, but I'm proud to carry it. I've often carried it alone, with occasional seasons when someone has been present for me — but I've never felt safe enough to fully let someone else help me carry it. I can unload a bit of it but never enough to fully breathe. After years of grieving combined with chaplaincy, I have a heightened awareness of when people are capable of being what I need and validating my story, instead of minimizing it or listening without empathy. I've noticed that fewer people have both the desire and ability to be fully present for someone in the way the person hurting needs them to be.

All the way back to elementary school, I can recall being the kid other classmates came to when they had problems. Oftentimes, those same kids would ignore me until they needed me again. My mom would frequently share her concerns that people were taking advantage of me, while also affirming me for my natural gift of compassionate listening. Sometimes, she'd say, "If you spent a little less time listening to everyone's problems and a little more time studying, your grades would be even better." I had good grades, but she wanted me to have great grades. She didn't want me to stop being that safe space for people — she simply worried it would take a toll on me and affect my own future. It seems she was already laying a foundation for taking care of myself while carrying the painful stories others shared with me. Helping people came to me naturally, and I believe I always knew my profession would be something focused on caring for people. It wasn't clear what that would be, though.

For Open House in kindergarten, we had to draw pictures of what we wanted to be when we grew up for all the parents to see that evening. My brother had the same teacher and did that project three years earlier. He drew Jabba the Hutt as his career aspiration, and my parents were hopeful my drawing might create a little less chatter among the parents. My classmates all drew teachers and doctors. I drew an ice cream man on a bicycle. Weird, right? Well, I think it was telling — and thankfully my mom was an artist and always encouraged our creativity. Every summer until we moved to Texas, my dad's side of the family would spend a week at Rehoboth Beach in Delaware. To be historically accurate, those trips occurred for over 50 years before our immediate family joined them and continued after we left. The four of us only participated when we lived in Pittsburgh. Each summer, I'd see a man riding a bike on the boardwalk. He had a huge metal cooler attached to his bike and a beach umbrella over it. He would sell ice cream out of the cooler, and I remember him bringing joy to people. That's what I wanted to do. I wanted to bring joy to others, and the only way five-year-old me could articulate that was by saying I wanted to be an ice cream man on a bicycle. For the rest of my childhood, I would freeze when asked what I wanted to be when I grew up.

Even in college, I couldn't nail down what I wanted to do. I loved French and other cultures, and I majored in Modern Languages and Literature, encompassing the literature of French, Spanish, and Italian. Languages connect people, and they allow us to enter other people's worlds. I loved that about them. Speaking other languages gave me opportunities to get to know people, places, and cultures in ways that speaking only my native language wouldn't allow.

In a way, this was still preparation for what was next, but the future wasn't yet clear. A few summer internships in secondary and higher education gave me ideas, and I chose to teach French and Spanish in a private school. It wasn't permanent, but it felt like a door to either a master's in French or skills for something else. It wasn't long into my first and only year of teaching that I felt called to seminary. I was well-supported emotionally and financially by my church to make this happen. I knew I didn't want to be a church pastor, but I trusted that it would become clear while earning my Master of Divinity.

I was able to take Introduction to Pastoral Care my first year, which is rare given the standard requirements for new seminarians. This course is essentially an introduction to psychology for clergy and others in ministry. It opened my eyes and excited me, and I felt like I belonged in the classroom for the first time in a long time. When my first paper was returned with a grade, the back page was covered in a note from the professor. I had math class flashbacks. The blue pen appeared red in my eyes because of the sheer amount of it — but then I started reading what it said. It was the most empowering, affirming, and motivating note.

That note gave me clarity and purpose. My professor shared that he recognized a gift in me for pastoral care. He had been a student himself when his own pastoral care professor — who turned out to be the author of some of the most important books on pastoral and spiritual care — saw the same gift in him and nurtured it. My professor became a mentor to me. He was a church pastor on Long Island during 9/11, and his experience caring for his congregation, many of whom lost family in the World Trade Center, was invaluable. He and his wife both had a Master of Social Work in addition to his Master of Divinity and PhD, and I later babysat their dachshund and daughter. As I took every class he offered, I dove into every aspect of pastoral care. After graduation, I was accepted to Clinical Pastoral Education (CPE) programs in the Texas Medical Center, and I completed an internship and the required yearlong residency to become a staff chaplain in a hospital. It wasn't long before I recognized a call and passion for pediatric chaplaincy, and I continued to advocate for its uniqueness — the knowledge of childhood development it requires — as my role evolved.

Chaplains are frequently asked to describe our jobs. I like to say that we help people find hope in a mess. Everyone finds hope in something, and I discover what that is and build a foundation of support from there. It's my way of being the ice cream man on a bicycle. We actively listen with empathy in ways that make people feel seen, heard, loved, and validated. We are companions through loss, trauma, and times of spiritual distress. And I love it.

Being a chaplain quickly became part of my identity, and anytime it felt under threat — which it did — there was grief and fear. I couldn't turn it off either. Whether I was at work, at the barn, or at the grocery store, if I saw someone crying, I had to approach them and offer help. I would listen and be what they needed regardless of how much it drained me. During my 44th year, I finally set a boundary around that to protect myself, knowing how difficult this year would be.

I am often asked if I became a chaplain because my mom died when I was young. I'd estimate that question has come up no fewer than 200 times, and I recently polled fellow chaplains to see if people name their own past trauma and grief and tie it to their vocation, too. Not a single chaplain who responded has been asked, "Are you a chaplain because of [insert major grief or trauma]?" I'm it. Why? If people already knew my mom died, they assume that's why I chose this career path. If they find out later, they ask. While I can see that they're making a connection, I hate that question. It feels like my expertise in this field is minimized and questioned — as though they think I'm trying to work out my own grief or trauma by taking care of other people. It appears I'm being accused of being less professional and authentic, and it creates a sense of shame in me. It's likely that none of that is intended by whoever is asking, but that's how it feels.

Women are already fighting for their voice to matter and to be as valued as their male colleagues. I have the added issue of being petite, which has been regularly used to put me in my place. I wonder if people used my mom's height against her the way they do to me. Like many women in chaplaincy, I have entered patient rooms to be met with, "You're not what I expected." After years of this, I turned it into a joke and would say, "Were you expecting an older man with grey hair?" They'd laugh and say, "Yes." Even in the early days of my career, I'd be turned away for being a woman, and some families would request a male chaplain. Thankfully, this happens significantly less often nearly twenty years into my career, and less in pediatrics than in adult medicine. I fought hard to be respected as a chaplain, and it feels as though equating my mom's death with my profession adds another hurdle — as if I don't deserve it as much as chaplains who don't have a dead parent, especially male chaplains.

There is no doubt that my mother's death has influenced my skills and abilities as a chaplain. But it is probably not a direct cause of my becoming a chaplain — because then everyone who lost a parent when they were young would be a chaplain, social worker, therapist, and the like. They aren't. Young grievers have every type of career as adults. I didn't become a chaplain because my mom died when I was young, but living without her has absolutely shaped me as a caregiver. I'm a better chaplain because of her death and my grief at a young age.

There was a chaplain at Mom's death, but I had no idea why he was there or what he did. Clearly his presence could not have made me say to myself, "I want to do that and help people" — the way kids do when they see a vet care for their dog or an ER doctor save someone on TV. It wasn't like that at all. In fact, the chaplain at Mom's death gave me a lot of lessons on what not to do. There's also no way for any of us to know what my profession would be if Mom were still alive. Would I still be a chaplain, or would I have discovered something else? My life could look completely different — and likely would. What I do know is that being transformed by grief at a young age made me a better chaplain than I would have been had I not experienced that. It was as if I were light-years ahead of others in empathy — in knowing what to say and what not to say to someone in deep, raw grief. I never left anyone to face the hard things alone.

One of my favorite interventions as a chaplain is bibliotherapy. I use children's literature to guide children in articulating their feelings, making sense of their diagnosis, finding hope and meaning, and processing their grief — whether over their own impending death or that of a family member. One of the books I use most is *The Rabbit Listened* by Cori Doerrfeld. In the book, a little boy named Taylor builds a massive tower out of blocks. One day, his tower comes crashing down. We can all relate to everything falling apart at once. Different animals come in with the intention to support Taylor through his tough time, but they each have an agenda on how to do it. They project how he should cope in their own minds — whether through talking, laughing, getting angry, or something else. Then, suddenly, a rabbit appears. The rabbit doesn't say anything. He simply sits and listens as Taylor goes through every emotion in his own time. The rabbit was present and followed his lead. He listened. He was exactly what Taylor needed.

Chaplains are trained to be like the rabbit. I have always been seeking people who could be the rabbit for me, and knowing what it feels like to need one has changed how I function as a chaplain.

I needed someone to listen without giving clichéd advice — or any advice at all. Chaplains don't solve problems or offer solutions. We're not fixers. We empower others to find a path, and I needed adults to be that for me. I needed someone to sit with me. I needed someone to make sure I didn't stop riding horses in college. I needed someone to let me cry. I needed someone who would let me express my emotions without calling me "sensitive" or "emotional." I needed someone who made me feel like I wasn't alone or abandoned. I needed someone to make me feel safe and loved. I give all those things to my patients and their families as a chaplain. I needed the rabbit. I became what I needed.

XIV

Giving Each Other Grace

THERE WERE, AND ARE, MANY PEOPLE who grieved the death of Debra Shannon. The primary three are my dad, my brother, and me. We may be grieving the same person, but we're grieving the version of that person that we each knew. There's some overlap, of course. We have to give each other grace in our grief processes. We cope in our own ways and on our own timelines, and that's okay. Sometimes, it's hard to accept and wrap our minds around how people can grieve the same person so drastically differently.

I have limited information on how my dad and brother processed their grief on their own. We rarely talk about her or our feelings with each other. I can't speak to how they grieve her on a daily basis, nor is it appropriate to judge or assume how someone grieves. I can, however, speak to my experience and my hopes.

We have never been together on the 12th of December, and I'm not aware of whether they do anything to honor the day. She is almost never mentioned on the rare occasion that we are in one place. If Mom does come up, most of the time, I'm the one who says her name first. My brother doesn't talk about her. He seems uncomfortable when I mention her in person or over the phone — as though the word "mom" is taboo unless it's in Korean to or about our dad's wife. If stories about Mom or other deceased family come up in texts, he's silent and doesn't typically comment on that thread. My dad will post vague references to Mom on Facebook that are almost always followed by a post about his current wife. Occasionally, he'll tell a story about her in our group text. While it may be part of my coping to bring her up every chance I get, it may be theirs to be quieter and reflect on their own. Perhaps saying her name hurts them the same way it heals me. My dad once told me that I "hug like her," and I instantly wondered if that had created some of our distance. Perhaps I remind him almost too much of her. While that can be difficult for him, the idea that I've become so much like someone I love yet didn't know well fills me with pride. Imagine hugging like someone you haven't seen, let alone hugged, in decades. I need to have the same grace, awareness, and understanding that I hope my dad and brother have for me as we handle each day and milestone in our own way. We need to be able to say, "She needs to talk about her. I'll listen," and "They need to post song lyrics or reflect on her quietly." It is so important to respect how each of us grieves the same person.

On the first anniversary of Mom's death, Dad sent my brother and me a heartfelt email that was unexpected yet beautiful. I was astonished, and then he did it again the following year. He'd write about Mom, and we'd learn about her. He would express love for us, and I would cry through it. I loved these emails and began waiting for them. The last email I remember was in year nine, but maybe there was one on the tenth anniversary. But one year, the email didn't arrive in our inboxes. He never wrote them again, and I don't know why they stopped. Those emails gave me hope for the three of us as a family, and they created conversation about our grief and Mom that was unusually vulnerable for us. I really hoped those emails would draw us closer together in our pain. There would always be some emailing back and forth for a day or two once that year's email arrived, and I loved that the conversation and connection were rooted in those notes from Dad. It broke my heart when they stopped.

Part of me assumed Mom's death would unite my dad, my brother, and me and ensure we would be incredibly close for the rest of our lives. That has not been the case. We are not closer because of her death, and that is okay. I've felt validated after learning how normal this is among other motherless daughters. Closeness and frequently sharing about Mom may have been my hope, but that isn't our reality. When one of us mentions Mom, it is fairly one-sided. We cope so differently, and we need to offer each other grace — and to engage in the ways that heal us individually.

When my brother was approaching 44 years old, Dad and I wondered if he thought about how significant that was. I don't recall if we discussed it with him or not. As far as I know, he didn't have a big grief math year when he was 44 or count down days and months to see how long he'd lived with a mom and without — but he might have. I did those things. That was, and is, part of my coping. Grief math is common, and I wonder if it is more universally calculated among young grievers who lost a same-gender parent.

Other big parts of my coping are talking about Mom, immersing myself in grief education, and teaching others about grief. Note that I didn't say "provide grief support." That is not part of my coping. It is how I help others cope.

I'm passionate about ensuring the bereaved have a safe space for their complex feelings, and I give them expert care built on all the grief work I've done on my own.

I talk about my mom a lot, and that includes arguments we had, traditions she loved, where she experienced God, and her death. I love to share all aspects of who she was. Chatting about her life and death heals me. I wish that my family spoke about her more, particularly without needing me to prompt the topic. There are few people in my life at this point who genuinely knew my mother, and I want so badly to share stories with them. I'd love to hear my brother's favorite stories of her, things he remembers her saying a lot, and what her favorite piece was that he played on the cello. She adored all of our hobbies, especially music and riding. It astonishes me that people who never met her are more open to discussing her than people related to her — but when I really reflect on that, I realize there must be a lot of unresolved pain there for them. To say a phrase I hate: it is what it is. The more I connect with a support group of motherless daughters, the more I learn that my story with my family is far from unusual.

Feeling like the only one who wants to talk about Mom reminds me of how lonely grief has been for me and how much of my grief work has been done on my own. Whenever I see a job description mention "self-starters," I think, "if you only knew." I made a conscious decision not to hide from my grief and to keep Mom's story alive. Thanks to my high school teachers, friends, and barn family, I was never afraid to open up. It was hard at first. I was used to being the listener and not the talker, and that was before I listened professionally. But I quickly learned that it's healthy and necessary to be a bit selfish when you're in raw grief. It'll pay off later. Now I regularly comfort people by saying, "It's okay to be selfish when you're grieving, because grieving isn't actually selfish. It might feel that way sometimes." It can feel selfish, because it's so difficult to advocate for what we need and feel heard. I knew facing my grief had to happen, or I'd be an utter mess. I am grateful for the handful of people in those first few months — including my high school best friend, my riding trainer, and my French teacher — who countered all the loud voices telling me to "be strong for your dad." The kids and adults at school and the barn were the exact opposite of the adults at church and in the neighborhood. Grief work is hard, draining, and full of every emotion possible, but I am thankful that I didn't shy away from it.

It's common for people in fresh grief to distract themselves from their feelings by immersing themselves in work and suppressing tears. I find comfort and peace in letting the tears come and facing grief head-on. Holding in our big feelings is like not wrapping your pipes before a big freeze. The pipes eventually burst and cause devastation. Grief can only be hidden for so long before it hurts you or someone else. I like to think of grief as love, because we don't grieve things we hated. Every time I tell a story about Mom, no matter how brief or detailed, I am saying, "I love you, Mom."

I hope this grief stays with me because it's all the unex-pressed love that I didn't get to tell her.

———

XV

Regrets, I Have a Few

M Y MOM DIED AT THE HEIGHT of middle-aged mother and teenage daughter drama. I vividly remember her telling me once that she was sorry for how critical and moody she was. She admitted she wondered if she was in early menopause but didn't think she could ask her mother about her history. I understood that more than she knew. Back then, perimenopause wasn't a word. She probably was in perimenopause, but her moods and reactions were likely also heavily influenced by a brain tumor we didn't know she had. We argued a lot. She was extremely critical of my weight in ways that still affect me. Our drive to the barn was 45 minutes, and one time we were so irritated with each other that we drove in separate cars. My dad stood in the driveway and shook his head in disbelief as we pulled out of the garage in unison — in our own cars — headed to the same place. Thankfully we typically drove together, and those 45 minutes were some of our best conversations. But I'll never forget the day the tension was heavy enough that the only option was to go separately.

At seventeen and eighteen, I beat myself up over every tiff Mom and I had, no matter what the root of it was. It could have been the most normal argument for a parent and teenager or one that began out of hurt, but I blamed myself. She wasn't there to blame. I was angry about every time I rolled my eyes or slammed a door. I felt guilty about each of those. I felt shame that I never got to tell her I was sorry, and she couldn't apologize either. I was sad that we were never able to heal from those issues — and I know, with certainty, that we would have. I grieve what could've been.

In the early months of grief, one of the books I was given discussed "grieving the whole person." The author encouraged bereaved readers to remember not only the great parts of the person who died — not to romanticize them — but to grieve and acknowledge the difficult parts and any unresolved conflicts. Those need to be grieved, too, because otherwise we can't heal the parts that complicate our grief. Every person has wonderful and harsh traits, and both make them who they are. I felt safe to share things Mom said that hurt me, until that girl in college shamed me for it — which simply told me she wasn't a safe person. Eventually, I relied on this concept to move past my guilt and shame about the last years of our relationship.

During that first year, I went through waves of guilt and shame — both of which are common in grief. When we express feelings of guilt, our friends and family often want to comfort us with statements like, "It isn't your fault" or "You did all you could." Those comments can minimize the guilt, though. We need permission to sit in the guilt and shame to get to the other side of it.

Recently, I was listening to a woman process "if only" statements about the decisions made in the days leading up to her mom's death. She said her husband and friends were telling her that she "didn't need to feel guilty." I asked her how that felt. "I feel like they're not listening," she said. I explored her guilt with her, validated it, and helped her reframe it. I let her feel it safely. She felt heard for the first time in weeks. I remember what that was like, and how it has shaped my ability to feel comfortable processing feelings of guilt related to Mom, jobs, my horse, grief over not being a mother yet, or anything else. Anytime I've felt shut down in processing deep feelings like guilt — especially as a young griever — I learned to withdraw. The lesson is either that those feelings aren't legitimate or that no one cares.

The result is suppressing those feelings, and that's a recipe for disaster. It has been crucial to face the feelings of guilt and shame while also accepting that my feelings of anger or hurt because of things Mom said or did were equally valid.

When I see certain pictures, they trigger memories that hurt. I want to go back to that time and calmly say, "Mom, I am sorry for how I reacted. What you said hurt, but I need to respond better." She could say the same. And then we could have a real chat. She was emotionally intelligent and patient, and those traits assure me that conversation could've happened if she had lived. But that can't happen. Now. We won't heal from those parts of our relationship.

When there are conflicts that aren't resolved before someone dies, it's complicated grief. There are many times I have thought, "If only she had lived a few more years — when daughters and mothers become friends — we would've been able to both say 'sorry.'" It's been just as crucial for me to grieve that stage of our lives as it has been to grieve the tiny gifts she would leave and the enthusiastic way she would redecorate my room to reflect my latest passion. Seriously. When I came back from Sea Camp in 8th grade, she had filled my room with fish pillows and replaced my 90s translucent phone with one that had an orca as a headset coming out of a wave as its base. It made whale sounds when it rang, and it was both horrible and hilarious.

While we had our arguments, we also built our great-est memories. We shared a horse who we all joked she loved more than us. A friend of hers once wrote me a note about her love for horses and their ability to connect us to God: "I also remember she loved her horses, almost as much as her family. She felt that animals were all part of God's world, which she truly loved through his Spirit. She was the best friend a person could have." Sharing a love for horses with your mom is an indescribable gift. She was the happiest she'd ever been, having finally owned a horse after dream-ing of it since she was a little girl — and she got to experi-ence that with her daughter. She loved my school and be-ing known as the one parent from the International Section who bridged the gap to the French Section. People con-stantly commented on how loving she was.

The tough bits were genuinely hard on me, and I imag-ine they weren't easy for her either. There is one thing that I don't have an ounce of guilt or shame about, however. I told her I loved her all the time.

———

XVI

Re-Grieving Losses

I AM FOREVER 17 while also being a middle-aged woman. That is what grief does to people who lost someone when they were young. I re-grieve my mom at every new stage of life. Like others who lost a parent young, I am permanently grieving — moving forward in the world without the person who was meant to guide me through every stage of it. It's like I'm frozen as a 17-year-old while also facing normal aspects of adulthood with a constant feeling that something is missing.

We don't move past grief but rather grow with it, and our losses feel new with each part of life we experience. When

I realize Mom can't listen to me work through whatever I'm dealing with or excited about, I'm reminded she's gone. I process her death differently at every age. When I add up my grief math to learn how long until I live half of my life with her and half without — exactly how many years, months, and days she lived, or what the exact day will be when I outlive her — I'm looking at her death through a new lens. As I reach milestones in school, explore college options, graduate, and maybe get married and become a parent, I face the loss of my sweet Mom again as if it just happened.

The developmental stages Mom missed for me encompass everything from turning 18 — old enough to vote but still very much a child in many ways — through leaving for college, my early 20s, full adulthood, and now middle age. Nineteen is an odd age. Many 19-year-olds live in dorms or apartments away from home and come home for holidays feeling as though they don't know what to do with their independence, while their parents are ready to hand them the chore list and ground them if they come home late. Family dynamics have a way of snapping back when kids in their late teens and early 20s return to their childhood bedrooms for Christmas and summer break. For me, grief was added to an already awkward phase of life. Every time I came home from school, I was smacked with memories of Mom while also adjusting to my dad's new life, new family, and new homes — first a townhouse, later a house in the suburbs. I needed her through every one of those changes. Her death was at the root of why they were so hard. I would chat with friends from high school and college, and we could all validate each other on how strange it was to head home for the holidays. I had another layer — or more — of pain that they didn't, and it was confusing and lonely.

As my grief math slowly added up, I felt like she left me again. At my high school graduation, I was filled with pride to hear that a scholarship for seniors pursuing creative arts had been created in her name — parents and teachers from my brother's class and mine had donated to it. My dad was able to present the first one, and it went to a friend of mine from Australia. I loved that she was being honored this way, and I felt like people truly saw her for the art-loving, kind, generous woman she was. But I wanted my mom to be in the room. I wanted to be annoyed at her demanding a million photos — not standing there without her, watching other mothers dote on their seniors. I wanted to be insulted by her saying I looked "chunky," because it would mean she was there. I wanted to roll my eyes at her as she stressed herself planning what she imagined would be an incredible graduation party. Instead, she was gone. She wasn't there. My riding trainer hosted my high school graduation party at her mom's house. I faced my first major milestone without her, and it felt like the loss happened that morning.

This has been an ongoing cycle. I thought of her as I declared my major in college, as my dad got married, as I studied in France, as I crossed the stage to grab my diploma and saw my brother on the other side with the family camera. I felt frozen at 17 while still taking on the world. No matter how many people showed me they loved me and were proud of me by traveling to Virginia for my college graduation or Austin for my seminary graduation, there was a massive void. She was the one I wanted there, and she wasn't.

Each time the loss felt new, I felt like a lost, lonely teenager. With every birthday — especially my thirtieth and fortieth — I wondered what she would've said or done to celebrate. My birthdays were exciting but also empty, and each one reminded me that the woman who gave birth to me had not been able to celebrate a birthday with me since I turned 17. She adored birthdays, and I do, too.

I continue to look at her death differently as I age. Regardless of age, bereaved people need connection — it makes them feel safe — and that's something I've craved since the moment I learned Mom was dead. It doesn't mean I'm stuck. Grief continuing means I'm healthy and in tune with my feelings and the loss. It is normal for grief to shift with us as we grow, but feeling as though the loss is fresh — like a miserable scene cut from *Groundhog Day* — is unique to young grievers. It's as if Mom dies again with each phase of life. It is terrible, yes, but also, I love it. I love it, because grief connects us to the person or pet who died. When I re-grieve, I find her again.

I am connected to my mom every time I reflect on her diagnosis, our last conversation, and her death. I am connected to her when I piece together memories from the short 17 years that I had with her. I am connected to her when I notice she is what's missing from every aspect of my life. I'm 17 and 44.

XVII

The Language of Grief

WHEN MY MOM FIRST DIED, people would say, "I'm so sorry for your loss" or simply, "I'm sorry." Why do we apologize when someone dies? I was a kid, and I wondered why people were apologizing. They didn't kill her. They didn't give her a brain tumor. Unlike the doctors, they didn't lie about her prognosis and give us hope that she'd be fine when they knew she'd likely die. I don't remember any of them sincerely apologizing, though.

It isn't unusual for me to say, "I'm so sorry you lost her" — or to use their name, or the relationship: wife, mother, daughter. When I say it, however, it doesn't land the same way it did when people said it to me, because I've thought carefully about the person first — their situation, what they need, what tone will reach them. It isn't my go-to response, and it isn't delivered the same way every time — it's tailored to the person and their loved one. I know when and how to say it in a way that validates their pain rather than just filling the air. Whether I say it at all comes after reading the family's emotions and how they're coping.

Sometimes, "I'm sorry for your loss" has an air of pity to it, and I don't want pity. I want to feel heard and comforted but not pitied. Words and body language that communicated pity told me that the other person didn't want to listen. It seemed as though they were uncomfortable, and they couldn't put aside that discomfort to be there for me. I was seeking — and still am — validation of my thoughts, feelings, and grief. I wanted someone to listen without trying to fix the situation with a platitude. Like most grieving children and teens, I needed emotionally present adults who showed me that grieving openly was healthy. I needed honesty, clarity, presence, connection, and safety. I didn't need pity.

"I'm sorry for your loss" is an apology, and the word "loss" can stick out sometimes. Many people argue that the word "loss" and all its forms should be avoided in grief language. We lose our keys but find them in the couch cushions. We lose our phone but hit that side button on our Apple Watch to find it. When a person or pet dies, we can't find them again the way we find our car keys and phone. That might mean they aren't really lost — but I'm on the fence.

I did lose my mom. I did lose my first horse. I did lose our four dogs. They are lost from my life, but I understand the argument to omit "loss" and "lost." It's why language is so crucial. The word works for me, because my mom is missing every milestone. She has missed 27 years of significant events and will miss more. She is missed, and I feel lost without her. Perhaps that's the real loss. The language of grief isn't about what is easy or comfortable for the person speaking. It's about what is age-appropriate for the bereaved and helps them cope. It's about what brings the griever comfort and lets them know they can trust you. It is always about them.

One word I don't like — neither as a chaplain nor as a griever — is "strong." I can't count how many times a parent has told me they "need to be strong for their kid," or how often a mother has said "I have to be the strong one in the family." As I've said, people also told me to "be strong for your dad," which meant to hold in my tears to protect him. Once I left for college, people stopped telling me to "be strong for your dad" and switched to saying, "you're so strong" because of how I've handled the loss of my mother.

That is a bit more accurate, but still not comforting or vali-dating. Hearing that I was strong — or needed to be strong — only shut me down, as it does for so many. I believe strong people talk, face their grief, and aren't afraid to ex-press their feelings.

We teach the children around us how to grieve by the way we grieve. I don't remember seeing my dad or my mom's brother — a weekly dinner guest for years and one of my dad's closest friends — cry, or hearing either of them talk about their feelings in the months between the funeral and my leaving for college. I wonder how our relationship, and our grief, would look if I had been able to see my dad and uncle as healthy examples of how to grieve. I wonder about things like that a lot, but I can't change my grief responses or anyone else's. Self-awareness helps. Noticing how lan-guage has made me feel since that dreaded night in Decem-ber 1998 has been healing — for the families in my care and for me. There's such strength in vulnerability, and the mis-use of "strong" when someone is hurting undermines their confidence to face their feelings and process them. It isn't strong to bury emotions and grief. I'm strong because I faced all of the sadness, anger, disbelief, and confusion of be-ing motherless and navigating life without my natural guide. I'm strong because I didn't run from grief. It matters how we use words.

Language is funny. I've always been fascinated by foreign languages, and I am now equally enthralled with the use of my own native language to express emotions, process grief, and support others in theirs. Some phrases are harmful to someone in grief. Some are comforting. Others are situational, or person to person. Thanks to chaplaincy, I am acutely aware of people's body language and always assessing their reactions to words and tone. Because of that, I adapt my language moment to moment and use what seems to help that person given what they face and how they cope. What comforts one person may be offensive to another, and I find that being aware, following their lead, and not having an agenda are the most compassionate approach. I want to be a comforting presence to people who hurt, just as I once wanted and needed — and that means I have to be wary of being so focused on saying what I think needs to be said rather than what they need to hear. It starts with listening and being fully present. I needed someone to listen, not project their coping or needs onto me, and show me that crying and sitting with some anger or guilt are healthy.

As my own grief has changed, so has the language I find helpful rather than harmful. I ignored platitudes in my teens and early 20s even though they confused, hurt, or angered me. I stayed quiet and suffered on the inside. Now I feel as though I can draw on my professional experience to gently challenge those platitudes. For instance, I used to be told,

"Someday, you'll see why this had to happen to you" — or "What lesson, or gift, did you get from your mom's death?" Yes. Those things were said to me as early as days after she died. I can now respond calmly and curiously: "And what reason — other than the medical one — do you think my mom died? What is the purpose?" They don't have an answer.

I do not believe that everything happens for a reason. There is no positive or non-medical reason that my mom died when I was 17. I wish people who say "everything happens for a reason" would also provide the reason, given how omniscient they seem to be. And then there are the faith-based platitudes — "God needed another angel" or "God needed your mom." God doesn't need my mom, and God certainly doesn't need her more than I do. The idea of my mom, or any of the children who died in my care as a chaplain, becoming an angel did not comfort me. Angels in scripture are typically frightening warriors. They're so scary that the first thing they say when appearing to someone is, "Do not be afraid." That's not a comforting way to think of my dead mom. I heard all of those phrases 27 years ago, and now I respond to them. I ask questions, then offer language that I — and other grievers like me — might prefer to hear. It's part of my dedication to grief education. I also thank the person for trying, because I give grace to their efforts to show they care. They never mean harm and are only trying to comfort me with the tools they have — and I want to use my experience to help them not hurt another griever in the future.

My mom's death is not a 1990s Aesop's fable with a moral to be a map for my life. Her death is not a lesson or a gift. When I was 17, people would tell me it could be just that. They seemed to think it would comfort me to be told there would be a great life lesson because of her death, or that I would create something magical out of the pain. That felt incredibly tone-deaf and cruel to hear. A lot of things were said to me that started with "at least," used the word "strong," or were full of confusing or hurtful metaphors. The language used shaped me. I've undoubtedly learned a lot from her death and my grief, and I believe my grief is a gift because it connects me to her. But her dying is not a gift. I'd rather her be here and lose every bit of knowledge I have about death, dying, and bereavement. Living all but 17 years of my life without a mother is not a gift. This isn't a parable or fable. It's my life.

XVIII

Grief is Cumulative

THE ROOT OF MY GRIEF is my mother's death, but I have been hit with many different losses since then, and they all affect each other. Cumulative grief is a reminder that grief isn't linear — new losses stack on top of older ones. Memories, pain, unprocessed experiences, and complex feelings resurface. These griefs — the deaths of my mom, my dogs, and my first horse, as well as losses of identity and community — all impact one another.

The first time I truly understood cumulative grief was when Dancer died. His death prepared me for the layers of grief that would surface with the deaths of my four dogs. When he died, I was broken and distraught. It was just shy of seven and a half years after Mom's death and a year before I finished graduate school. I knew it would be hard to lose him because I shared him with my mom, but I didn't anticipate the way it hit me physically. He represented so much. I don't recall who said it, but someone at my seminary named it. "It's like losing your mom all over again," they said. Bingo. Nailed it.

I can still hear the sound of Dancer falling to the ground after he was euthanized. The vet said I didn't have an option, and I was thankful not to have a decision to make. I ached. Two of my professors suggested there be a memorial service for him. My seminary Greek professor had a horse farm outside of Austin, and he sent his regrets for not being able to attend but included Scripture he always read when one of his horses died. He added his interpretation of the verses and how they apply to bereaved horse people sending off their beloved horses. I wish I had his email stored somewhere, but it's long gone. A group of students and professors gathered in a large patch of grass behind our main academic building. We sat in a circle, and one person read the words sent by our professor. Others led songs. We worshipped. I cried. It was the first time I felt fully seen in my grief. They gave me a service that honored the life of a horse who had united my mom and me and given us both such joy, love, and confidence. By doing so, they honored my mom and our relationship as mother-daughter horsewomen. It almost felt as though I was getting a do-over on her service and had a say in it this time. I felt so loved that day.

Someone simply saying, "It's like losing your mom all over again" woke me up to cumulative grief — for the people in my care and for myself. It sparked a self-awareness about future losses that has helped me immensely, and naming cumulative grief has validated a lot of complex feelings for bereaved families. Once we have had one major loss, every future loss brings up the first and all the others, and being aware of that can give peace and clarity to the pain. Cumulative grief slapped me in the face with the force of a Category 5 hurricane in 2022, but a bit of backstory is necessary first.

My family's home was always full of dogs, and the way my parents taught me to see dogs aided me later as a bereaved person and chaplain. My dad taught me how to make our dogs and cats a priority and treat them like the family members that they were and are. My mother taught me to see God in them and to become closer to God by spending time with animals. We had many conversations about being a voice for animals, having a heart for them and protecting them, and finding God's peace in their spirits. She would talk about God's magnificence seen in horses and encourage me to watch them at play in a pasture to truly see it. Her face glowed around horses.

A lot of families have dogs, and a lot of people consider themselves dog people as opposed to cat people. My family cherished all our animals. In my mind, we were not simply a family who had dogs. We were a family because of our dogs. What was ingrained in me was that animals would always show me love and teach me how to love others. When stressed, anxious, or afraid, animals would be there — the calm or the silliness, whichever was needed. They are always what we need, just as God is. Dogs and horses embody the same energy, love, joy, peace, and playfulness that I aim to offer the patients and families in my care. They mirror us as chaplains mirror their patients. To me, dogs and horses are sources of hope. I'm not sure where I'd be without their companionship and love.

The year 2006 started with the deaths of my childhood cats and Dancer. Those deaths fell every other month, almost to the day, between January and April. Like the deaths of other family dogs earlier in my life, these three losses were a harsh reminder of the loneliness of disenfranchised grief — but that pain was nothing like the grief Patrick and I would later endure together. The cats, despite my being a dog person, were living with me in my tiny graduate school apartment. They had been added to our family when I was in elementary school, if not before. After a lot of research on the ideal dog for an active person with no idea how long it would be before a house with a yard was possible, I welcomed a Boston Terrier in October of that year — a breed known for being a devoted companion, endlessly adaptable to any home. This dog would play, cuddle, and hike like the best of them. Oliver Austin, a four-month-old Boston Terrier, entered my life and became more of a best friend than I could have ever imagined. To this day, he is the best friend — human or otherwise — I've ever had, and people commented regularly on our bond. My fiancé still remarks on how he's never seen a relationship between a human and a dog like that. He likes to pretend that Oliver sings Heartland's "I Saw Her First" to him about me, and he continues to do that when we tell stories about my sweet Ollie.

My family never had one consistent breed of dog, but Oliver turned me into a Boston Terrier mom for life. One of my childhood cancer patients, who nicknamed me "Super Chap" and even had a custom superhero cape made with that nickname emblazoned on the back, once told me that I was "the human form of a Boston Terrier." That was one of the greatest compliments I've ever received. If anyone feels the joy of a playful Boston Terrier or the healing peace of one cuddling close after spending time with me, then I've followed my call as a chaplain well. Funnily enough, I love to refer to my beloved thoroughbred as "the horse version of a Boston Terrier." A few years later, after a long walk around Houston's Memorial Park, Oliver and I met a dapper attorney named Patrick and his two beagles, Daisy and Lily, at a local dog park. Daisy and Lily were a year younger than Oliver and checked every beagle stereotype. Oliver made me into a Boston Terrier addict, and I wanted my own Boston pack. Once the beagle girls entered our lives, it seemed crazy to add a fourth dog to the mix. It was so much fun to have Oliver at home and the girls at least a few times per week — but there was a hole that could only be filled by a tuxedo-wearing cartoon character.

In January 2010, the tiniest Boston Terrier joined the pack, and we named him Buckley. I'm forever grateful that my fiancé not only validated my need for more Bostons but made it happen. He grew up in a house with dogs, but he didn't fully transform into a dog person until we met. Buckley seamlessly went from his litter to our pack, and the pack now felt whole — and perfectly symmetrical. I walked all four at once with the Boston boys on my left and the beagle girls on my right. It was quite a sight!

On our walks through every neighborhood in which we lived, it was not unusual to hear comments from other people out running or walking their own dogs (and occasionally from moving cars) — their shouts were less than creative and rather tiresome after a while. They'd shout, "That's a lot of dogs!" or ask if I was a dog walker. One man, however, once yelled, "That's a lot of grief!" I countered with, "It's a lot of love." Years later, we were reminded of his comment when three out of four of the pups died within nine months. It was 2022. Daisy was fourteen and a half years old and left us in January. Oliver, my soul dog, was three weeks shy of turning 16, and his death shook me. He died in May. Lily was fifteen years old when she died in September. Both Lily and Oliver died suddenly at home. Buckley was suddenly a solo pup for the first time in his life. He grieved while being a source of coping in our grief.

Two years later, in February 2025, Buckley died of a collapsed trachea at fifteen years old. His death shattered us.

That's a lot of grief.

Dancer connected me to Mom, and he helped me cope with her being gone. Every time I was with him, she was there. I could feel her. His death felt as though she died again. Daisy and Lily's deaths bookended Oliver's. When Daisy died, we hurt for her, and there was an ominous feeling in the air. I knew it was the beginning of the end of the pack I called "The Texas Pups." They even had a classic canvas L.L. Bean tote bag with "Texas Pups" monogrammed on it that we took on their many road trips. They traveled to New Mexico, Santa Fe, the entire Gulf Coast, and the East Coast all the way up to Washington, D.C. The Texas Pups went to New Orleans so many times that they knew when we got to Audubon Park. They relaxed at cafés in the

Garden District and the French Quarter while I had a po-boy and their dad devoured a bowl of gumbo.

There was no way anyone could've predicted how quickly they would die one after another. Oliver's death was a nightmare that I frequently replay in my head, and I would do that no matter how he died. That morning, I woke up to two photos of him and me at the Grand Canyon in my Facebook memories. I reposted them with a caption about how I "never repost Facebook memories." I kissed his nose, told him I loved him, and left for work. As I was comforting a family whose baby was dying in the NICU, I received a call to come home. My boy was gone. Buckley held on for two more years, and it wasn't easy. The Texas Pups helped me cope with career woes, grief, and everything else that came along the way. Along with Gunner, my thoroughbred who became my heart horse in 2020, they were a safe space for me while I was a solo chaplain during the COVID-19 pandemic. Our walks were the only place it was acceptable for me to cry about the deaths and traumas of the infants and children I cared for as a pediatric chaplain. They gave me permission to be human when my profession required otherwise. They were my source of joy and hope, and their deaths added layers to my grief. Their deaths changed me as much as their lives.

Four months after Buckley died, Stewie was adopted from South Texas Boston Terrier Rescue. He was four months old, meaning he was born the same month Buckley died. He's a brindle Boston Terrier who is brilliant and sneaky. Like my horse, he was named after Arsenal F.C. Arsenal are the "Gunners." Stewie, or Stuart, is named after Stuart MacFarlane, Arsenal's photographer. Although Gunner and Stewie have yet to meet, they are both unpaid grief professionals. I survive cumulative grief because of them. I survive reminders that my mom is missing because of them. I survive the deaths of the Texas Pups because of them. That's a lot of cumulative grief.

———

Left Behind

WHEN TAYLOR SWIFT'S *MIDNIGHTS* album was released, I burst into tears the first time I heard "You're on Your Own, Kid." We won't even discuss the buckets of tears I've shed listening to "Bigger Than the Sky" from the *2am Edition* or *Evermore*'s "Marjorie." As I heard her voice naming something I'd carried alone for years, tears began to fall. By the time the song ended, I was sobbing. I pulled my car over. I felt like I couldn't breathe. In my abandonment and loneliness, I felt seen.

For the most part, my grief process has been a solo endeavor. In fact, I used to tell people, "I basically had to raise myself after my mom died." My dad traveled a lot for work and left me alone in the house, and I left for college out of state eight months later. After I left the house — and even while I was still there, finishing high school — it was pretty rare for my dad to ask how I was coping or feeling. We talked about her when I still lived at home but not much after I moved out for college. I wanted so badly to be surrounded by other kids who were grieving, too, but I couldn't admit to my dad that I needed to go to the local children's bereavement center, because of other adults' instructions that I be "strong for your dad." You'll never hear me say anything remotely close to that to an adult, let alone a child. It became clear to my high school friends that I needed to speak with someone professionally, and we had a school psychologist on our campus a few days each week. I was scared to go. I went to her door once, stood outside for a few minutes, and left. My best friend wouldn't let that happen again. He walked with me, knocked on the door himself, and sat on the couch with me for a few minutes until I appeared to feel safe and relaxed. He then excused himself, and I began visiting that psychologist once a week for a while. It helped. Years later, however, my stepbrother went to that school for a short time. He had an appointment with her, and he told me that she shared she had supported me through my grief.

HIPAA, anyone? My stepbrother used that information to hurt me rather than have empathy for what led me to see the school psychologist. Trusting a therapist after that was almost as hard as trusting a doctor ordering an MRI for my headaches.

I truly felt like I was on my own. Grief books mentioned that the bereaved often have feelings of abandonment, and that was confusing to me at a young age. Every time that topic was addressed, I'd think, "Mom didn't choose to leave me. This doesn't make sense." In the early days of my grief, the idea of her abandoning me angered me. She would never do that. Sure, she once forgot I had an orchestra concert, missed the whole thing, and didn't pick me up until an hour after it ended — but she would never abandon me. I wanted to scream at the authors of the grief books, "She didn't leave me by choice!" She did leave, but not in the traditional sense. I slowly realized what abandonment meant in terms of my own grief: the possibility that I had been left by the adults in my life to grieve on my own, and that abandonment can lead to attachment.

My mom left me to live without her example. She left me to navigate the end of high school, college, and the rest of my life without her. She didn't decide to leave or get in her car and never look back. She died — but it can still lead to feeling abandoned, especially for young grievers still understanding the world and themselves. Losing a parent young shakes up the world of the child left behind, and nothing ever really seems right again. The void is heavy, and we can feel angry and discouraged at being left to handle life on our own.

Sudden death can increase feelings of abandonment even more. The day my mom died, I woke up thinking I'd spend time with her at the hospital and the rest of the day at the barn. Instead, I rode my horse and headed off to a concert at a Houston club before being summoned to the hospital. The next time I saw her, she was dead. Our conversation the day before was nothing unusual — except for the location, her being in a hospital bed, and her obvious physical pain. We didn't have tearful "I love you" exchanges, and she didn't give me encouragement or advice for my life. We thought we'd see each other soon, and life would go back to normal. But it was never normal again. She left me to handle life without her love, guidance, and support.

While I did not completely understand what grief books meant when they discussed feelings of abandonment, I was later able to see how it manifested in me — because her death was so unexpected, and I was just 17. I would easily and quickly become attached to friends, boys, riding trainers, and coworkers. It always felt like I valued friendships more deeply and quickly, because I needed the closeness those friendships gave. When I'd learn that friends in college would walk right past my room to go eat in the cafeteria together but wouldn't ask if I wanted to come, I would think they no longer liked me. I'd spiral and analyze every recent interaction with them to figure out how I'd hurt them, even if I clearly hadn't. If my friends went to bars in Charlottesville or Lynchburg without inviting me, I'd feel deserted and unwanted. Many people feel left out when their friends are together and don't include them — but my responses were heightened. I'd post a vague status on AOL Instant Messenger or try to get their attention dramatically. I was in constant fear that everyone I cared about would leave. When they made the effort to include me, even for chicken fingers in the cafeteria, I felt seen and loved. I also felt reassured of their presence. They weren't going anywhere. On the other hand, if I heard them giggling as they walked by my window, I would be crushed. It's a good thing social media didn't exist then, because I can't imagine how I would've responded to seeing them all post photos in their Instagram stories at a boathouse party while I sat in my room wondering where everyone was. I eventually learned this was all rooted in feeling abandoned after Mom's death.

I had to live each day and make decisions without a mother's counsel. She was gone. She left. She can't dance to ABBA with me anymore as we laugh and cry through *Muriel's Wedding*, watch that wild galloping scene in *The Man from Snowy River* with our jaws dropped to the floor and tears in our eyes, and she can't make a little string horse for me to pretend I'm Elizabeth Taylor in *National Velvet* as she pretended she was riding in her little twin bed. She is gone, and I feel left behind. And I was scared that everyone else would do the same. I constantly fear that those I love will leave, and I feel like I've had to handle so much alone.

Each time "You're on Your Own, Kid" comes through my car speakers on shuffle, I cry, and I let out a huge breath. I've handled this largely on my own. I felt abandoned by her death, and by being left on my own to make sense of it. I felt abandoned by the adults in my life who left me to figure out grief before I learned how to vote. My mom survived a lot when she was growing up, and perhaps she passed that resilience in the face of abandonment and loneliness to me. There may not be a trophy for it, but I've done it. I'm on my own, kid. And I can face this. I always have been.

Missing From Me

MISSING SOMEONE WHO DIED LOOKS differ-ent over time. My mom was 4'11" and weighed about 95 pounds, but she left a massive hole in our lives. I immediately missed her presence in the house, even the bad bits — because every aspect of her personality made her who she was and made her my mother. With each grief math problem, what I missed changed.

Whenever I tell my mom I miss her, I always say it in French, even though she didn't speak it. She loved that I did, though. In French, "I miss you" is *tu me manques*. The direct translation is "you are missing from me." If that doesn't describe the void left by someone who dies, then I don't know what does. And that is why I prefer to say, *"tu me manques, Maman"* into the air every so often. It isn't to sound chic. It is because she is missing from me. Part of me left with her. I like the image of a bereaved heart as a mosaic — something beautiful made from broken shards. Our hearts are pieced back together but never quite the same. Something is missing from us, but we find ways to move forward while always carrying the awareness of that loss.

Initially, I missed her as my mother. I even missed the half-full cans of Coke she would leave in the fridge. She'd say, "It's too much. It's like a piece of cake. I can't finish it." We would tell her it would go flat sitting in the fridge waiting for someone else who might only want half a can of Coke, too — but she kept doing it. What I wouldn't give to be irritated by a wasted can of Coke, even though I don't drink it anymore.

It was immediately clear that she was the glue of our family and the creative, thoughtful source of all our family traditions. Those faded quickly after she died, and that stung. Seeing Christmas and Thanksgiving meals no longer requiring a dress code was one of the first changes I noticed. One by one, each tradition she built fell apart, and the home she created turned into a house. It was nothing without her leading it, and how much she did for us was evident now that all that love, attention, and silly celebration were gone with her. In tenth grade, I didn't have a date to Homecoming, and I was at a new school. I invited a friend from my old school to join me, but we didn't have plans to go out to dinner before the dance. We figured we'd eat whatever my dad cooked that night. We were getting ready in my room when my mom knocked on the door with a dish towel draped over her incredibly sculpted arm. She had good arms before it was cool for women to have strong arms. In a horrific French accent, Mom requested, "Please join me in the dining room of Chez Shannon." She even tried to make our last name sound French by how she pronounced the "non" at the end. Downstairs, she kept up the charade as she served us food — my dad played chef, she played waiter — and they giggled in the kitchen. There was no one else left who would create spontaneous moments like that to make me feel loved. I missed her joy and her ability to make even the tiniest moments feel monumental. Perhaps that's where my desire to honor every milestone of grief math — as well as achievements of all sizes for the people and pets in my life — comes from. My dogs and horse each get full-blown birthday parties with homemade treats and silly hats, and I know that was an example set by my mom.

The house was so quiet that I even missed our arguments — the ones that seemed terrible but were probably pretty standard for mothers and daughters. I missed singing in the car to Garbage and The Cure together. Each holiday came with buckets full of memories of her that made me miss her deeply, including her reputation for designing incredible Halloween costumes. One of the children's hospitals where I served as a chaplain had an annual Halloween event, and I prided myself on unique costumes the kids loved that could also be adjusted for sensitive situations. One year, dressed as Mary Poppins, I thought of Mom with every step while dancing the entire "Supercalifragilisticexpialidocious" almost exactly as it's done in the movie. My dance partner was a Chick-fil-A cow.

As the years added up, I missed different parts of her. First, I missed the person she was that I never got to know. I wanted so badly to reach that stage of life where mothers and daughters become friends, and I found myself a mixture of sad and jealous while witnessing my friends reach that phase. Our dog-walk chats had begun to shape our relationship into what I imagine it would be now. Sometimes she spoke to me like a friend on our walks, and years later I thought she might have been laying a foundation for how we'd evolve as mother and daughter as I grew up. When Mom first died, I was incredibly irritated by people who were mad at their moms or complained about them. They had no idea how lucky they were to have something to be upset about — because their mothers were alive. Later, I'd hear friends chatter about their regular coffee dates with their mothers and how much help their moms gave them, both emotionally and financially, while simultaneously complaining about boundaries. What I'd give for my mom to be alive and have horrible boundaries.

The closer I got to her age, I realized I didn't know who I missed. I remembered so little of her that I could no longer say, "I miss when Mom ___." There were snapshots — not screenshots; those didn't exist when she was alive — that I held on to. I wondered which stories were real, which had been told so often because they were the only ones I could confidently retell, and which ones I had unknowingly elaborated on to fill the gaps. People would say, "You must miss her so much." I absolutely did — but probably not in the ways they assumed. When you remember so little of a person, what you miss after nearly thirty years is not the same as what you missed in the first days, months, and years.

The first years were full of missing parts of her and our family when it was whole. Soon, the moments she missed were glaring. Everything that a mother would be a part of, she missed. My grief math pushes me to count how many Christmases, Thanksgivings, Easters, and birthdays she missed. She missed all my graduations, career highs and lows, and meeting my fiancé. She would love how smart he is, how much he reads, and how much he shapes his life around dogs. His bipartisan political impersonations would have her in stitches, and I would love to hear her laugh like that. Most of all, she would love how he advocates for me. I often think about how she missed meeting and loving my dogs and horse, and she would laugh that I call her "Grandma Bee" when I talk to them about her. Debra in Hebrew is "honeybee," and my dad called my mom "Bee" instead of "honey" as a term of endearment. I like honoring that by referring to her as "Grandma Bee" to her four-legged grandchildren. I've noticed Gunner grow calm whenever I ride him on December 12 and tell him that today is the day Grandma Bee died. Mom was the one who taught me how to put animals first and see God in them. We once sat on the top rung of a pasture fence together and watched Dancer graze and play. She pointed and said, "This is where you'll feel closest to God." That moment felt vulnerable and beautiful, and I'm grateful it's such a rich memory.

Twenty-seven years later, I miss what could've been. Now that I'm the age she was when she died, I miss having a guide, the confidante I knew she would've become, and the greatest barn buddy I could have. I wish I knew which parts of me are from her life with me and which parts of me are because of her death.

I miss what was. I miss what would've been. I miss what could've been. *Tu me manques, Maman.* You are missing from me, Mom.

Family Changes and Dynamics

I WON'T GO INTO TOO MUCH DETAIL about my dad, his wife, her son, and the family they built. I will, however, discuss how it felt to watch it take root and grow, as vulnerably as I can. The emotional and spiritual distress children experience when their surviving parent remarries is common enough that even the Christian satire show *Righteous Gemstones* tackled it.

My dad was 43 when my mom died, and they had been together since meeting in ninth grade. As I grew older, my mom slowly added more details to their high school dating story when we chatted about it — but the part that never changed: they met in art class. Dad's sister and brother were out of the house when my grandparents and Dad moved from Pittsburgh, PA to Avon Lake, OH. My parents met not long after, and both were students at Avon Lake High School. Their houses were three blocks apart. My mom was the oldest of eight kids, and her youngest sibling was 14 years her junior — meaning he grew up knowing my dad as well as he knew his own brothers and sisters. They were the epitome of high school sweethearts, and I remember being very aware that my parents were in love while I grew up. I wasn't aware how rare it was until friends — from the barn and from school — commented on my parents' loving treatment of each other.

After Mom died, a couple of my friends told me that one of the reasons they liked spending time at my house was because of my parents. Others agreed. "It's so obvious your parents are in love, and it's nice to be around that." My friends' comments both shocked me and made me proud. Years later, when Dad remarried, I often caught myself making sure everyone knew my dad and his wife met after my mom died. This thought didn't occur to me right away. It was a response to my own confusion when people asked if they were married before my mom died. The idea that my ridiculously in love parents would ever end their marriage by choice was unthinkable. No! My dad adored my mom.

The way he loved her taught me what kind of love to accept for myself. I couldn't let people think that for even a second. I stopped using the word "remarried" quickly and focused on phrases like "got married again recently." I stopped starting sentences with "My dad and stepmom," because, given their reactions, that phrase gave people the impression that my parents divorced, my dad remarried, and then my mom later died. I made sure everyone knew the timeline — partly to honor my parents' marriage, partly to honor my mom, and partly to communicate that our home wasn't broken until death came.

A lot of kids in my high school didn't know what to give me when Mom died, and a bunch of them hit the grief aisle at local bookstores and picked out some top titles. It was a lovely gesture. They were trying, and it was clear. One kid in the class below me dropped off an entire plastic bag of grief books at my house, with a card about not knowing what words to say but wanting to help. I read every single book my classmates gave me. One of the themes across nearly every book was about parents remarrying after their spouse dies.

Again and again, I read statistics regarding marriage after "'til death do us part" became a reality. According to the books, women either never remarried or waited a decade or so to find a new husband. Men, on the other hand, were typically married within two years. Dad and his wife got married two years and two weeks after Mom died. In one of our arguments early in their marriage, I remember telling him he was "textbook." Yes, arguments. Neither of us handled him building a life with his wife and stepson well. We both made some mistakes. He's my dad, though, and I want him to be happy. Even though I immediately knew he would marry someone else, it was beyond difficult. I didn't get a new mom. Why would he get a new wife? But that wasn't why the situation was so hard.

I never really felt like my dad was replacing my mom to forget her. What was strange is that I didn't have a lot of people attempting to comfort me by saying, "He's not replacing her." Just the opposite. People of all ages would say, "I know people marry again after death, but I never thought your dad could love anyone like he loved your mom," and "I bet it feels like he's replacing her." I'm not sure why people said that to me. There's a long list of things that people said during the early years of grief that still surprise me. What's even more surprising is that teenagers said more comforting things and created more space for me to talk than adults. Adults said one offensive thing after another. The "replacing your mom" comments didn't resonate with me. I knew there was no way anyone could replace her. When it comes to my dad's dating and remarriage, it wasn't that it happened — I expected it. It was how fast it happened, how in the dark I felt, and how my brother seemed to have no reaction at all. It wasn't long before he was calling her "Oma," which is "Mom" in Korean. I never felt like my dad replaced my mom, but every time I hear Nate say, "Oma," it feels as though my brother replaced our mom. I feel like he forgets our mom a little bit more each time he refers to our dad's wife as "Mom" in her native language. That may not be the intention, but it's how it feels. It's the opposite of clapping to help a fairy get her wings.

I left for college in August 1999, eight months after Mom died. My dad stayed home, and my brother drove me to Virginia on his way to Pittsburgh, where he was studying at Carnegie Mellon. I didn't return home to Houston until Christmas break, and, like the holiday season before it, it wasn't all that joyful. Our second Christmas without Mom — the conductor of our Christmas traditions and celebrations — was another confusing holiday full of new things I couldn't really wrap my mind around. Nothing was the same. With her gone, I needed some normalcy to help cope with her absence, but that wasn't an option.

My dad sold our home and moved to the opposite side of town. After riding my horse one day, he asked me to stop by the old house for something. It hadn't closed yet, so it was technically still ours. I stood in our empty living room, and the emotions were overwhelming. I hadn't seen it without furniture since we moved in in 1991. It felt dark — not the light-filled home of my childhood — but her presence was strong in that house even without the furniture and dé-cor she had picked out. It was somehow haunting, though. I could see her walking around, but the emptiness made it cold rather than comforting. I was angry my dad sold it, though. I needed to come home to the place that was full of her memories and presence. It was too soon and too many changes — but it made sense for him. I can't imagine how lonely he felt in that house.

On Christmas Eve, my mom's brother came over to my dad's townhouse so we could all go to church together. He and I rightfully assumed we were going to Grace Presbyte-rian Church, a church we'd been members of for years. We were standing by the front door, waiting to get in the car, when my dad said we weren't going to Grace. We looked at each other in shock. Dad said we were going to a Korean church he'd been attending — where he had been teaching an English-speaking Sunday school class. That's the way he described it, with no other details. Neither my uncle nor I were pleased, particularly as we were learning this as we were stepping out the door. So much of our lives had changed, and we wanted something normal and comfort-ing. We wanted to hold our "Silent Night" candles in the church where Mom worshipped weekly and where her fu-neral was held. The safety and comfort of my church made me feel at home. My uncle only attended Christmas Eve with us, but he liked the traditional service and spending that powerful night with us. We both felt like something that gave us peace was being taken away — just like so much else. It made sense if my dad needed a new weekly church home, but my uncle and I needed what normalcy we had left on Christmas Eve.

During the service, a woman came in a little late and entered the sanctuary loudly. I was used to quiet Presbyterians who, if arriving after a service started, waited until an usher silently nodded for them to enter, then crept to a pew. She squeezed by other people in the row and sat down next to us. She leaned over to me and said, "You must be Debbie." At the sight of both my uncle and me staring wide-eyed at the stranger who had just called me by my dead mother's name, she giggled and said, "Oops. I mean Jessica." We weren't introduced to this person. As we sat in silence, listening to a sermon in Korean and wishing we were on the red plush pews of my home church, I noticed something else. She was wearing my mom's black skirt with the little yellow flowers. Let me repeat that. She called me by my dead mom's name, and she was wearing my dead mom's clothes.

The changes were too much. Home wasn't home. We were just getting used to a life without Debra Shannon. I couldn't take it. I contacted one of my closest friends — my brother's best friend — and told him what was happening. He was at his mom's house in Belgium, and I was pet- and housesitting for him and his brother. They found someone to check on the house in my place and invited me to Brussels for New Year's Eve. I got on the first flight I could find. I escaped.

Not long after ringing in the year 2000 in the Grand-Place of Brussels, Belgium, I returned to Virginia for my second semester of freshman year. Between Christmas Eve and my return to Houston for the summer in May, I never learned who that woman on Christmas Eve was. There was no introduction or mention of her. Naïvely, or because I was out of the loop, it never crossed my mind who she could be — and my dad never said a word about her.

That summer, I got a retail job at one of Houston's malls, the Galleria. One day, my dad strolled into the store, holding that same woman's hand. My grief brain was fully engaged as the only thought that came to mind was, "She must be lost, and Dad is helping her." There is no logic in that sentence, but there isn't a lot of logic in grief. Our minds frequently protect our hearts. Seconds after my dad and the mystery woman left the store, my Crabtree & Evelyn colleagues, who were both in their 50s, cooed, "Your dad and his girlfriend are adorable." Wait. What?

My brother may have received better communication about Dad's dating life than I did. That's always possible. I know I was never told, "This is my girlfriend." After a while, it was simply clear. It was, once again, too much. Dad finding someone new to love wasn't what was too much. It was the lack of communication, care, and compassion. He had every right to meet someone, and I had every right to hurt. In my family's eyes, I was the problem, though. I packed up my car and headed north. I spent several weeks at my uncle and aunt's house in Maryland, then couch-surfed in the Washington, D.C. area, staying with college friends from Sweet Briar and Hampden-Sydney who were there for summer internships, until the dorms opened at Sweet Briar. Being at home in Houston had become lonelier and heavier than I could handle.

In Virginia, change was welcome. It was part of college, moving from adolescence to adulthood, and full of hope for our futures. The changes in Houston were disorienting. Home wasn't comforting. Mom was gone. The house belonged to someone else. Dad had a new life. It was too much — and everything Virginia offered felt safe and hopeful.

My dad, my brother, my paternal uncle and his family, and I spent Thanksgiving 2000 at my paternal grandparents' house in Ohio. It was a busy holiday, but it was the first one where I felt everything was slowly healing. My mom's absence remained an elephant in the room, and I eagerly waited for any family member to talk about her. Thankfully, anytime I was alone with my paternal grandmother, she would find a way to tell me how much she loved my mom. I didn't think it was possible to admire her more, but her rare vulnerability with me made me feel closer to her and love her even more deeply. It finally felt like our holidays were full of joy again. That was until the phone call.

My uncle drove my dad to the Cleveland airport. We said our goodbyes, with plans to see each other at Christmas. My uncle returned to my grandparents' house, and the phone rang seconds after he got back. I remember how he looked at me as though he was expecting the phone to ring. He answered it with an eye on me. It was for me. My dad was calling from the airport, and he had something to tell me. We'd spent a few days together, all in the same home, but he called before boarding to share his news. Holding a landline, standing in my grandmother's TV room with family shuffling about, I heard words I didn't expect. He was getting married on New Year's Eve. Between his wedding date and Thanksgiving, we had the second anniversary of Mom's death, college semester final exams for my brother and me, and Christmas.

On the last day of 2000, my dad became a husband again. His wife's eight-year-old son was a ring bearer. As people were arriving, I said something to the same friend whom I had spent New Year's Eve in Belgium with the year before, and he said, "Whoa. You sounded just like your mom there." I don't know what I said, but apparently my inflection stopped him in his tracks.

My dad's wedding was another change. We knew the day would come, but it was another chapter in grief and a new normal. Within two years, my mom died, I started college, I lost the comfort of my childhood home, two dogs died, and we watched my dad get married. The latter was a happy occasion for my dad, and for that, I'm thankful.

The first years of their marriage were not easy for my relationship with my dad. At first, she tried to befriend me by taking me shopping and buying me lots of shoes and handbags. When we were alone in their house, she would pick at me. I would respond, and she would tell my dad. My dad would, in turn, tell me how horrible I was. My perspective didn't matter. I was the only one who could be at fault. When I was at their house, I slept on the floor in his home office or on a couch separated from the kitchen by only a shoulder-height counter — and Dad would start tinkering loudly in the kitchen next to me in the early hours of the morning. I felt unwanted.

Later, I learned that I was unwanted in a couple of ways. Close friends of my dad told me he was toying with "cutting me out" because I was not skipping around the house as if his wife and stepson were the greatest things to ever happen to us. It didn't matter how they spoke to me. My stepbrother once told me he was glad my mom died so that he could have my dad. There were times when it appeared my dad's wife and I would be okay. We were almost friends, and I had hope. She no longer seemed to be turning my dad against me, and everything seemed pleasant. One day, that stopped. We both quit working on the relationship. I wasn't invited over to the house anymore. I wasn't aware of anything that happened to cause it, but I only saw my dad at restaurants. One time, my dad called me from the airport and asked to stop by my house. I was thrilled. He sat on my couch with my fiancé and me, and the three of us decided to go grab lunch at a local Tex-Mex spot. Before leaving, my dad called his wife to update her on his delay home from the airport. We could hear her yelling at him through the phone. He wasn't supposed to spend time with us, and we didn't know why.

The responsibility for the health of our relationship was placed solely on my shoulders, and others blamed and judged me without truly reflecting on the situation and everyone's roles in it. I grieved alone and was expected to smile and nod. That isn't realistic, loving, or fair. I have learned that strained relationships between daughters and fathers after the mother of the family dies are not unusual. For years, I carried guilt, anger, and sadness that we weren't the father-daughter pair of my childhood. I realized it wasn't me. I've released it. My dad is happy and loved, and that is enough.

I have lived motherless since I was 17 years old, and I will be motherless for the rest of my life. Like many motherless daughters, witnessing our fathers go from happily married

to widowers to married again shakes our reality and our family of origin. Each one of us hopes our dads are happy, but
there is a part of us that prays that happiness can come in
ways other than finding a new wife. No matter how old we
are, we still want to think of our dads as deeply in love with
our mothers — while also finding comfort that our fathers
are loved by someone else, ensuring they can share their lives
with someone. It's quite the paradox, and it is rooted in
love. I will always find peace and comfort in the love my
parents had for each other, and I am grateful that my dad is
not alone. He is loved, and, as long as he can take deep naps
with dogs and experiment with new recipes in the kitchen,
he'll have joy in his life.

———

XXII

Sliding Doors

NYONE WHO HAS HAD A SIGNIFICANT LOSS in their life is forever changed. There's a distinct before and after — a personalized BC and AD. While we can see how our lives have unfolded without our loved ones by our sides, it is normal to wonder what could've been had things been a little different. What would have happened if her tumor had been discovered earlier, or, better yet, if there had been no tumor at all? Where would we be?

I wonder what my life would look like if she hadn't died. If those twelve days in December had been altered by even a second, my family's life — both collectively and individually — would be completely different. Would my profession be the same? I'd undoubtedly still be in a helping profession, but would I still be a chaplain? Would I be living in France or England as she and I predicted? She'd hate that I'm still in Texas. She would fear that meant I was stuck.

There is one part of my life I know she'd be utterly pleased about — enough to forgive me for not spending my adulthood in Europe: my animals. If she were here, she'd love to learn what absolute cuddle bugs Boston Terriers are, and she'd laugh every time I describe them by saying, "They're like cartoon characters." The beagles would've found her lap the second she sat down on my couch for our regular teatime that we would most certainly have. She would also be thrilled to get to know my horse, Gunner, and she'd likely have adopted a thoroughbred, too. She'd be just like me in finding purpose in giving a thoroughbred a second chance instead of getting a warmblood solely because that's what's more respected these days. When Oliver, Lily, Daisy, and Buckley died, she would've been present for me in a beautiful way, and I can only imagine how much Stewie would've entertained her.

I'm confident we would be close. I wonder about her life just as much as my own — what would it have looked like, had she lived? She talked about flipping a house in the Houston Heights. Would she have done that, or would she have had land, able to see our horses from her porch? She'd certainly be surrounded by horses and dogs in some way, and I hope she'd have found time to draw and travel. She had such a love for art that she had been rediscovering in the last couple of years of her life, and drawing the dogs gave her such pride. She would've retired the second she could — to dote on my niece and nephew and ride horses through Ireland.

This sort of wondering is part of grief math, too. Sliding doors moments make us reflect and think of "if only" and "what could've been," because grievers may need or crave some control of their reality. We need to dream a bit. All my dreams and imaginings of what could be are rooted in the love that Mom had for me and that I had for her. Sometimes, realizing that none of that is true can make us sad — but sometimes it can fill us with gratitude for the memories we were able to share. We grieve the dreams of what could've been while grieving what was. Reflecting on what our lives would look like is a healing part of grief math that gives us permission to hope. Hope is what gets us through it all, and I am always seeking moments that fill me with hope. Hope allows me to live a life full of love and empathy, just as she did — even if it looks completely different from what it might have been if Mom were still here.

XXIII

"You're So Much Like Your Mom"

IN THE YEARS FOLLOWING MY MOM'S DEATH, people started telling me, "You're so much like your mom." They would never elaborate. I only knew her as a mom. Before she died, she was beginning to give me a window into her life before my brother and I were born and introducing me to bits of her non-mom personality. There was so little I knew about who she really was.

She told me how much she loved emailing with my brother once he moved away for college. She said they were becoming close and developing a whole new relationship. I remember being hopeful we'd find that someday. Despite her sharing more about her true self, we still only knew one version of her.

The comments never came with any explanation, which left me to imagine what they meant. The Debra Shannon I knew claimed she couldn't work "because the cat is in my lap." She constantly commented on her teenage daughter's weight and would say, "Do you need to eat that?" She loved to work in the yard, go for dog walks and runs on her own or with our greyhound and Airedale terrier, and ride our horse. She was incredibly unsatisfied with her job. She loved the Lord, had a deep curiosity in other cultures, and was creative. She rarely cooked, loved animals, and seemed to enjoy writing chore lists for her kids that somehow always included "pull weeds." She loved classical music and singing The Cure, Garbage, and The Cranberries. Now that I am the age she was when she died, I can see how I am like her at this age. I used to adore my career and see it as a vocation. Now, after years of being borderline obsessed with my vocation, I'm suddenly unsatisfied and unfulfilled with it just as she was at 44 years old, but perhaps we aren't meant to be fulfilled with our careers as long as our personal life fills us. The more I channel chaplaincy into writing, however, the more content I feel again. Also like her, I'd rather split my day between dogs and horses and sprinkle in occasional international travel. For the longest time, though, I had no idea what people meant when they said, "You're so much like your mom." Was it an insult? Was it a compliment? What characteristics did we share? I decided to ask.

During the summer of 2007, I was in my Clinical Pastoral Education (CPE) Internship prior to my yearlong residency. In addition to a Master of Divinity, CPE is required to become a chaplain. We were each tasked with coming up with a project that would force us to process something heavy in our lives. Part of CPE requires us to explore our past traumas and grief to ensure our stories don't negatively impact our patient visits. This intern project was the first of many ways I had to tackle my own spiritual and emotional distress, as well as my past.

The project I set out to do was a bit risky and took some sleuthing. My goal: get to know Debra Shannon. I wanted to understand who she was other than being a mother. Who was she? What did she love? What did people love about her? What made her light up? I wanted stories, and it meant trying to find people she knew since elementary school at a time when Facebook was the only social media source and my mom's address book was long since gone. There was a chance I would learn nothing at all. There was also the chance that I would discover things I didn't want to know, needed to know, or would be thrilled to know. If there was at least one response, then there would be at least one new bit of information about her that I hadn't previously known.

My project began by making a list of people who were important to my mom. She had seven siblings, and I don't believe I put all of them on the list. Her sisters were certainly on it, and I already saw one of her brothers regularly. He told me stories about her with ease, especially when I invited him out for the annual December 12 dinner on the 25th anniversary of her death. I felt so close to my mom and him that night as he regaled me with stories of my mom as a teenager as we ate at a Tex-Mex restaurant near my childhood home 25 years after she died. My relationship with most of my aunts and uncles was not what I hoped it would be when she died. After her death, I assumed that her mother and her siblings, particularly her sisters, would smother me with love and attention regardless of geography. I expected my aunts would want to mother me to honor their sister. I anticipated they would be calling, visiting, sending care packages to college, and ensuring that there were women related to my mom guiding me through my next stages of life. That isn't what happened. Her mother was worse, which honestly shouldn't have been a big surprise but still was. She disappeared from my life almost instantly, and when she was reportedly asked how many grandchildren she had, she no longer included Nate and me in the total. I saw her twice after my mom died, and both times were by accident. She was visiting my paternal grandmother when I arrived at the house. One time, she mumbled "hi," got up, walked past

me, and left. She was always odd and far from trustwor-
thy, but her disappearance from her grandchildren's lives
after their mother, who was her firstborn child, died was
still shocking. Given her behavior, I didn't even consider
putting my maternal grandmother on the "to contact list."
I can't say for sure, but I don't think I put her four brothers
on the list. Only one of her family members wrote to me,
and that letter was not as healing and helpful as the ones
from her friends and neighbors. There was little about her
in there and a tone that was unsettling to me when it first
arrived, but neither bothers me now. It is honestly rather
fitting that her family had the least to say about her.

The rest of the list was filled with people who knew my
mom in different phases of her life. I wrote an artist who became friends with her during elementary school when they
were paired up for square dancing in gym class. If anyone
figures out why we all had to learn square dancing, please
feel free to let me know. Another person I wrote to lived
in our neighborhood in Pittsburgh. She ran into another
old neighbor of ours at a grocery store and told her about
my project. She gave her my address, and they both wrote
me. I had not spoken to either of those women in over 15
years, but their letters were some of the most impactful ones
I received. I sent a handful of letters to people in Louisiana
where I was born but have no memory of given we left when
I was still in diapers. My parents often spoke so highly of the

people from that phase of their life, and it was essential that I tracked down some of the old residents from Baker, LA. I wish I had kept a tally of how many letters were mailed from my little apartment near the Texas Medical Center to people Mom cherished from different eras of her life.

I wanted to know what people meant when they said I was like her. I often wondered, and still do, how you become like someone you didn't know and hadn't seen for years. If you don't remember the sound of their voice or their mannerisms, how do you become like them? I reread the handful of letters that were sent back to me in response every year. I'm starting to think that maybe they're all right. Maybe I am like her.

The things people said about her paint a picture of a woman who loved her family, friends, and Jesus with abandon. She was a listener and incredibly generous. She made people feel special and loved. Without changing their grammar — or much of their spelling — I'm sharing some quotes from the letters from her friends dating back to the early 1960s. Perhaps you'll be able to imagine what it would've been like to have Debra Shannon in your life. That's certainly what I try to picture.

"a kind and generous person. Always laughing and caring."

"...taught us so much about God"

"She was bubbly, outgoing, sensitive, fun, loving, caring and much, much more. When you had a conversation with her, she made you feel like you were the most important person. She was such a good listener."

"You asked what made her light up? Well, naturally, you and your brother made her light up. She was so happy to be your mother. You could tell that she felt as though you were a gift from God. And she treasured spending time with you. Your father also made her light up. They had such a good marriage."

"I think the reason your mom was always so happy was because she had such a great relationship with God."

"...liked to tease her..."

"Your mom worked hard behind the scenes but didn't like to take credit for her work. She was a very humble person. She was always ready to help others. We have a feeling you are a lot like her."

"I can only assume she might have possessed the skills of a sensitive vigilant observer even as a child."

"Even at that age I felt safe around her — most likely I wouldn't have been able to express it then. But I know that's what guided me."

"The last time I spoke to Debbie I do remember thinking to myself that I was in the presence of a remarkable person. It was a feeling of being accepted. I knew deep down that if I ever had to talk with Deb about the most personal

thing — she would just listen — with compassion, care and without judgment. In fact, I suspect she was able to be present in such an active way that she could take on the pain of the person she listened to. I would hear it in the inflection and the tonality of her voice when she responded to what I was telling her."

"My other strong recollection of her is the story she loved to tell about the girl in 3rd grade who accidentally pooped her pants...Deb got such a kick out of telling that story — that every time I talked to her — we would reminisce and eventually she would bring it up!...I loved to hear Debbie laugh when she would tell the final part..."

"She started dating a boy named Dan Shannon who I also hung out with on occasion. I remember seeing them often in the hall walking together. Debbie carried what seemed to be all of her books with both arms down low in front of her waist. She was short and petite and had bright brown eyes with a huge warm smile. Her hair was deep black and I think she parted it to one side."

"You would think that Debra Bedell was my biggest fan the way she would talk about all that she was impressed by in regards to me being an artist..."

"I was reminded of her undying care and concern for anyone that she allowed into her heart."

"Debra Bedell was rare — in the fact that she was open, maybe even vulnerable at times almost childlike. She had a spirit that was like warm energy. Now that I think

about it you could see that light and feel it — sort of like putting your hand through the rays of sun as they shine through a windowpane. She lived that brilliance — it was sewn with golden thread into the tapestry of what she was."

"Debbie was an exceptional human being. She seldom talked about herself — the focus was for the most part on you, your interests, and what you were up to in life. I see that now in reflection. I am sure she had her dark moments; maybe she hid them thinking they were not important. Maybe she thought it was not worth burdening someone by revealing another aspect of her personality — or maybe she only let her immediate family see those sides of her."

"Debra Bedell in my remembrance was an extraordinary woman and friend. Her generous spirit, deep caring, humor, love, wonder, openness and courage are uncommon in many of us. We can at best only aspire to have all those qualities. Most of us will finish out our time here only acquiring some of them. I can only surmise that someone like Deb who's light shines so intensely can only offer it for a short time. Let us hope (that is if you believe in the sweet hereafter) that she has returned to some distant star from where she came bringing that brilliant luminescence with her. In some other confounding way — who knows — it could have been her heart. Some of us can only take so much of the world's grief or the pain from others. I can imagine her heart just gave out — splitting open under the pressure of all that it absorbed."

"I cried as I read that you wanted to get to know your mom. In that way, how alike you are to your mom. She truly sought to know people and understand their inner thoughts."

"I will always remember her fervent dedication to God, to learning, and to the arts. She thoroughly enjoyed watching children grow and learn. She loved music and people."

"I remember most her laugh and her facial expressions when she saw the kids do something funny or when they made some small achievement. She was always encouraging."

"She never let on that she was suffering in any way...her strong point, even though I sensed that something was troubling her. She always was a good host and a listening friend."

"Your mom was a caring, generous friend. I knew I could always count on her to help me."

"...she would light up a room and exude happiness wherever she went."

"Mrs. Shannon was someone we admired because she had brought joy and togetherness to all of us regardless of nationality, she was our best ambassador we had from one section of the school to the other."

"...the thing I'll remember most about Deb — her laugh. It would always make me smile, even when I was low. It was a wonderful laugh. She had such a friendly out-

going personality, that upon meeting you couldn't help but like her. She was fun. She was bright. She was gentle. You never had a dull conversation with Deb. She truly cared about her friends. She was always there for me when I needed support."

"I hope for you and your brother that you experience life to the fullest as she did and do it with her joy and generosity. She made the world a better place."

"I don't think there was anyone more compassionate, tender-hearted and Christ-like in her care and concern for others in her love and obvious enjoyment of her very own family."

"I close my eyes and see a delicate lady with a strong spirit. I see her tiny busy hands and feel the love from her giant heart. I hear her wonderful laughter and I find myself smiling."

"Sometimes we are lucky enough to have a friend in our lives right when you need her. A friend that you could share secrets with, joys, concerns, child-raising stories. A friend that you trusted to listen and care. Your mom was that for me."

I can only hope to be like her.

XXIV

The More You Don't Know

WITH EACH DEVELOPMENTAL STAGE OR AC-COMPLISHMENT, there was a noticeable fig-ure absent to help mark the occasion, but the lack of Mom's guidance left a bigger hole than her joy at throwing another graduation party or expressing pride every time I spoke at a chaplain conference. My mom was not only a mother to me, and she would grow to be more. She was a teacher, a guide, and a safe space, and her absence left a hole that no achievement or milestone could ever fill. The age of the child and relationship to the parent certainly has an impact, and I wasn't immune to this consequence of early loss.

My mom loved a good theme and a way to honor every moment. I miss that. I miss her wanting the food to match party decorations or even the movie. I miss her creativity. But I want her guidance more, and maybe that is because I carried on her ability to recognize every milestone. She'd praise how I make food for every Super Bowl that represents the two cities that are playing, and I even attempt to get beer or wine from those spots, too. I'm always looking for a way to make people feel loved and highlight special days or accomplishments of all sizes. I do that because she did.

I don't know if I can emulate a mother's advice. That isn't the same guidance. It was those daily bits of advice that a mother gives her daughter that I needed so badly throughout my life, including makeup tips, how to get tough stains out of gentle fabrics, and what to bring as a hostess gift. I've Googled all of those things and more while simultaneously being the person my friends go to for the very etiquette advice my mother would have bestowed upon me. She loved etiquette and ensured I knew where her copy of *Emily Post's Etiquette* was in the house just in case I needed to reference it like an encyclopedia (spoiler alert: I looked through it for answers to questions I would've asked her many times after she died).

Every once in a while, a woman would enter my life and offer some of the motherly presence I needed for a bit. Time, distance, or drama would eventually end those relationships and stir up feelings of abandonment unless there was a natural end or shift in that relationship, but I kept trying to forge new friendships with women who were older than me but outside my family. For years, I sought the example of women in their 40s, and that didn't begin to shift until my great-aunt died and left me with no family matriarch. Mom was frozen at 44, and I wanted the support of people in her age group. Now women in their 40s are my friends and me. They're my contemporaries. Mom feels like a contemporary to me, because we're both 44. Soon, I'll outlive her, and she'll always be 44.

The women in my family, except for my paternal grandmother and paternal great-aunt, were not present in my grief. My grandma and great-aunt were from a generation that didn't speak about their feelings, but they would occasionally tell me stories about my mom while the rest of my family didn't say her name or check on me. It was very clear they were present in my grief more than their Anglo-American instincts would allow. Other aunts left me alone. I needed a woman to help me navigate life like a mom would, but no one loves you like your own mother. I figured that at least her sisters would step in to care for me, as my mom undoubtedly would have done the same for their children if the roles were reversed, but that was not the case.

I am reminded of the loneliness of not having a mother each year on December 12. I would reflect on the year and what she missed that year, and I would think about the hurdles I faced. I would wonder how she would've supported me and what advice she would've given. In the early stages of grief math, I wanted her advice on which college to choose. The summer before she died, she insisted that she wouldn't give her opinion on any of the schools we toured, because she didn't want to influence my decision. I would've wanted to sit on the futon in the game room with her and run through my pros and cons for each even if she wouldn't give her thoughts. She died before I sent out applications. Throughout college, I watched my friends go to their mothers for advice on everything from relationships, friendships, internships, help with summer housing, and jobs. They received care packages that I'm certain my mom would've sent, too. I bet Mom's care packages would've each had a theme.

When I got engaged, I was elated but also felt like I was robbed of sharing dress shopping with my mom. My sister-in-law and niece helped via FaceTime from Korea while two friends accompanied me. It was joyful but not what I dreamed, even though I'd been too young when she died to have ever pictured that day with her. I needed her advice but perhaps not the criticism that would likely have come, but if the criticism meant she was there I'd have welcomed it.

I had some lace from her 1970s wedding dress sewn into the back lining of my dress as if she is putting a hand on my back.

There are long lists of topics I wish I could've sought her counsel on or, at a minimum, used her as a sounding board. Any of my close friends can attest to how I love to process my decisions out loud, and Mom would've been a great teatime companion, barn buddy, and dog-walking partner to listen while I worked through whatever decision I was facing. She'd know when to offer advice, when to share personal experiences, and when to merely listen.

I'm at yet another phase of life when so many women turn to their mothers and ask about their experience at the same age. They ask their moms how they controlled their hot flashes and what other symptoms they experienced. I'd love to ask my mom when she began perimenopause, and she'd be fascinated to see how openly it's discussed. I'd ask question after question to learn from her, just as I would've done my whole life.

I often hear bereaved people in my personal and professional lives discuss how hard it is to not be able to pick up the phone and call their mothers. That's never been something I yearned for, because that wasn't normal for me. I still lived at home in a pre-cell-phone age. She was downstairs. I didn't call her. Even when I spent summers in France as an exchange student, I would only call to check on the animals but not to ask her for advice. I did share stories of my adventures, and that's not quite the same. I can't tell her stories anymore, and I wish that were possible. I want her guidance, and I want to be able to tell her stories — mundane and wild — but I don't relate to the desire to call her. It wasn't my norm before she died, but maybe yelling "Mom!" from upstairs tracks more with us. After 27 years, I don't always notice the deficit of Mom's advice until I witness someone my age chatting with their mother about the exact thing I'm wrestling with without Mom, or I come across an Instagram post of a moment that I wish were part of my own equation. That's when I think, "Oh, I needed Mom. How lucky they are." There are other situations I face when needing her is much clearer, including endometriosis, perimenopause, barn dynamics, and zipping up a white dress that seemed meant for me.

We divide life into stages — by number and by milestone — and my grief math reminds me that Mom is subtracted from each of mine. I am always without her compassion, generosity, and empathy. I celebrate others but have to extravagantly hint that I'd like the same. No matter how much I miss her smile, her gentleness, and her support, I know that her love is never far from me.

XXV

The Year Before the End

THE GRIEF MATH WAS BEGINNING TO GET SCARY when I turned 43. All of 2024, I was acutely aware that my 44th birthday was coming. It was on my mind constantly. Those around me saw a woman who was excited about her birthday and eager to tell everyone that her horse's birthday was two days away. I love that our birthdays are close together. Inside, however, I kept thinking that the end of my life was a year away.

It is hard on a daydreamer to sense only doom rather than the exciting things that could come. Almost all my report cards came back with notes about me staring out the window or daydreaming. My mom would get on my case about it, but I think she secretly loved that my imagination was so strong. She certainly wanted me to focus and learn, but she normally encouraged me to be as creative and imaginative as possible. When I was about preschool age, Mom helped me write my own books on her typewriter to give to the neighbors, and I remember one was about a couch that came alive while I was napping on it. My daydreaming understandably shifted to different topics as I aged, but it never faded.

A supervisor I once worked for tasked the team to read the same book to discuss our work styles. I can't remember the name of the book, but I'll never forget the new label that was stamped on me: "future thinker." That's basically the adult version of a daydreamer, and the definition hit home.

A future thinker is always planning far ahead. On the positive side, the planning (i.e. daydreaming) creates goals and motivation, but when those goals aren't realized, it hits hard. I can become deeply sad and discouraged when a major milestone or dream does not come to fruition. I have learned how to cope with the disappointment, and I stretch myself by setting achievable goals to help reach the big one. I used to plan every minute detail of the end goal. I could see a year, five years, further ahead, but I couldn't see how to get there. Pushing myself to look at smaller details to limit disappointment and maximize my daydreams becoming reality has been real growth. It worked beautifully until 2024.

I kept thinking how lucky I was to be 43 yet how afraid I was to turn 44. Instead of my usual excitement for the future, grief math filled me with fear and anxiety. That year felt like it had an invisible countdown clock, and any remaining hopes or dreams I had for my life needed to be completed before I reached 44 years, 9 months, and 6 days. Because my mom only lived that long, I was convinced that was my timeline, too.

I leaned into my daydreaming — into being a future thinker — and turned it toward my bucket list. I became more determined for Gunner and me to reach our first horse show. We'd had a lot of setbacks with trainers, my confidence, and figuring out his health. That dream came true on Gunner's birthday, two days after my 44th birthday and a week after our dog, Buckley, died. Gunner was a star at the show, and I felt like we were unstoppable. We also created some barn aisle chatter when people walked by as my barn's groom and I were singing "Happy Birthday" to my horse while he wore a birthday hat on the first day. That tiny show we did gave me enough hope that I began daydreaming for Team Gunner again. I also decided that I would do everything in my power to go riding in Ireland when I was 44, even if it meant taking on another job to cover the cost — which I did.

Regardless of how scared I was about what was to come after 43, I relied on my daydreaming and future thinking to cope with the grief math. If the math was correct, and I wouldn't live past 44, I'd make certain my last year was full of joy and hope. I'd spend that dreaded year creating memories. There's only so much we can control about our days, but I was determined to make the best of the alleged last year of my life.

I don't want regrets if I live for 44 years, 9 months, and 6 days or for 100 years. I work with people who are dying or grieving someone who died. Neither the dying nor the bereaved ever say that they wished they'd accomplished more in their career or spent more time at the office. They express satisfaction with their life because of experiences, pride in their children or spouse, and peace about having shared their lives with the people they love. I want to be able to list the cultures and countries I explored, the animals I loved and was loved by, and the people who filled my life with silliness, love, and compassion. I want my life to look like a series of daydreams that came to life with a few conquered obstacles along the way.

XXVI

The Second Worst Birthday

BIRTHDAYS HAVE ALWAYS BEEN A BLAST for me. My mom's creativity in organizing birthday parties was stellar. It was fun to collaborate in the party planning and watch her themes and excitement come to life. Her joy in celebrating birthdays was contagious and made me feel deeply loved.

When I was turning 6, I was oddly determined to have my birthday party at Denny's. Why? I don't have a clue. I wasn't, and still am not, a huge breakfast food person unless

I'm in Europe and surrounded by divine pastries and a classic Full English (or Irish) Breakfast. At age 6, a bowl of cereal was fun, and now my pre-riding fuel is fresh berries and yogurt. But for some reason, Denny's had to be my birthday venue, and there was no talking me out of it. Accepting defeat on the location, Mom was as resolute as ever. She reserved a back room at the local Denny's (I still don't know how I knew that existed), and she put all her energy into it. Instead of "Pin the Tail on the Donkey," she made a giant paper plate to hang on the wall. She cut out bacon and eggs from construction paper, and she spun a handful of kindergartners around for us to pin the breakfast foods on the plate. Everything was breakfast-themed. She took my weird idea and ran with it. Mom knew how to make everything fun and special.

Rather than lose enthusiasm over an upcoming birthday as I aged, I actually tried to extend my birthday into a Birth Week or even a Birth Month. I'd start daydreaming in January about different types of parties with various groups of people in my life and sometimes risked worlds colliding by inviting people from work, barn, school, and other spots to mingle. In the weeks approaching my birthday each year, I felt Mom in me — the best of her, shining through — even as my grief math began making me anxious.

In 2025, however, I did not want my birthday to come. I was full of fear, uncertainty, and dread. I was turning 44, and I always knew that it would be the second worst birthday I would ever have.

My worst birthday was my 18th. That milestone should be fun. I would finally get to vote and be considered an adult, even if I didn't feel like one. I should've felt hopeful turning 18 and knowing high school was coming to a close. There is such anticipation with turning 18. It's as if all the doors are opening at once, and I would get to write my own edition of *Choose Your Own Adventure*. 18 symbolizes choices and independence, and I looked forward to it for months. When Mom died, I didn't want that birthday to come anymore.

In the fall of 1998, my friends started turning 18. One by one, we honored a big moment for each of us. While celebrating my friends, everyone in my family was looking forward to my own 18th birthday. Months before, Mom even began asking what we should do. She was thrilled that my brother's 21st birthday was in mid-December, followed by my 18th birthday in late February. Goodness, she loved birthdays, and it's apparently genetic. Unfortunately, our mom died a week before my brother's birthday and two months before mine.

When February 1999 rolled around, a couple of friends wondered what we would do for my birthday. There were a couple of other classmates with birthdays close to mine, and we'd had parties together in the past. Would we do that again? Would we have our own parties? Do I want a big party or a small one? Normally, I had dozens of ideas about parties, whether it was for me or someone else, yet this time, I had none. They weren't used to prodding me with questions about my birthday. By the time my special day arrived each year, they were probably annoyed by how much I talked about my birthday. That, however, was not the case as my 18th birthday approached. Much to the dismay and confusion of some thoughtful friends, I had absolutely no excitement about my birthday.

For the first time, I felt anxious about my birthday. It felt heavy and sad. I was dreading it. A couple of friends started suggesting things, and I rejected every idea. Finally, I found the words. I stared at my best friend and said, "How can I celebrate my birthday when the woman who gave birth to me is gone?"

My birthday had been looming, and it wasn't clear why there was no joy in it coming. When I could eventually name why I suddenly hated my birthday so much, there was a bit of relief. Being able to ask, "How can I celebrate my birthday when the woman who gave birth to me is gone?" was freeing. Once that was said out loud, I could deal with the feeling.

Begrudgingly, I agreed to let my friends plan my birthday. It was a compromise. They knew how important birthdays were to me in the past, and once again, kids were proving to be better support in my grief than adults. They were forcing me to face my birthday, because they believed it was not only good for me, but what I would want under normal circumstances. But "normal" was gone. What was normal? Even things that were routine when she was alive no longer felt normal without her. Meals, despite her not being the cook, were weird and uncomfortable. Getting ready for school wasn't the same, and doing homework felt like a waste of time. Going riding was healing but her absence at the barn was heavy for everyone there. Those were all normal activities, but they felt anything but normal. A fête? How could that be possible now? Turning it over to them was the best I could muster, and I'm grateful for their efforts and desire to be present and loving in every way they could think of, starting the day after she died.

My friends picked Mai's, a Vietnamese restaurant in Houston that had been popular for ages. My memory tends to be insanely detailed, yet I remember only two snapshots of my 18th birthday dinner: my friends gathering in my living room to shower me with gifts before leaving for dinner and sitting at a crowded table at Mai's. I don't remember if I enjoyed it, felt numb, loathed the evening as much as expected, or a combination. I only remember that on my worst birthday, my friends did everything they could to make sure I felt loved.

Twenty-seven years later, on February 26, 2025, I celebrated my second worst birthday. I turned the age Mom was when she died. For at least a year, this birthday was on my mind. My 18th birthday only felt terrible for a couple of months, but the impending 44th felt ominous for quite a while. Like many adults who turn the age their parent was when they died, I carried a lot of uncertainty about what this year would mean. Would I also die? If I live longer than my mom, then how do I know what life looks like for a woman past that age? What examples do I have, especially with shared DNA, of what aging looks like? How do I celebrate a birthday when I'm scared? Those questions, and more, were on my mind almost constantly. While I anticipated that birthday to be terrible, there was no way to know just how awful it would be.

Four days before my birthday, our Boston Terrier, Buckley, died. He was the last of the Texas Pups. The grief over his loss was debilitating and cumulative. It was grief over him. It was grief over the whole pack of pups. It was grief over the end of an era of having the greatest dogs making my house a home. Any comments about how amazing it was that he lived over 15 years were not comforting, just as they hadn't been when Daisy died at 14.5, when Oliver died three weeks shy of 16, and when Lily died at 15. Buckley was gone. They were all gone. It was the first time in 18 years and 4 months that I didn't have a dog to race home to, explore the neighborhood with, or be woken up at a ridiculous hour for breakfast.

1999 was repeating itself. At 18 years old, I forced myself to go out to a restaurant for my birthday. In my grief, I let my friends take me to a restaurant while I stumbled through a celebration that no longer made any sense. In 2025, numb in fresh grief yet again, my fiancé and I walked like zombies into the dimly lit dining area at Xalisko in The Woodlands, TX.

My original plan for my 44th birthday was to take Buckley on some sort of adventure, spend as much time at the barn with Gunner as possible, maybe buy something fun for myself or go get a mani-pedi, and then dinner with my fiancé where he'd likely resist all offers to try my dessert because he was more than aware of the power of my sweet tooth. He has a talent for making me feel loved over special dinners, whether it's for my birthday or Mom Day. Intermittent tears were expected, but I only expected them to be rooted in the grief math of turning the age my mom was when she died. Instead, my eyes were puffy from crying from the profound and sudden loss of a beloved pup. The dreaded day was shaping up to be worse than imagined.

Despite the loss, the day didn't turn out terribly. I intentionally chose a Mexican restaurant to honor my mom's heritage. We were a little more adventurous by dining at a traditional Mexican restaurant as opposed to Tex-Mex, and the food was extraordinary. The heaviness of Buckley's absence was certainly palpable. I hadn't celebrated a birthday without a Boston Terrier since 2006, and it felt empty. Gunner proved, once again, what a gift in grief he would be.

I woke up the following morning knowing that everything would be different from now on. It felt the same as waking up the day after Mom died. It was similarly full of uncertainty and the unknown. Will my 44th year be the same as hers? Will I outlive my own mom? There was one surprising feeling on the ultimate grief math birthday, and it happened at the barn. Riding is an almost daily activity for me. When I settled into my saddle at 44 years old, I felt closer to my mom than I ever had — even though she's been gone for nearly 30 years. She was with me.

I didn't feel her around the barn, when I tacked up, or any other time. It was the moment that my left foot stepped into the stirrup, I swung my right leg over my horse, and I sank into my saddle. It felt as though she was in the saddle with me. I paused. It was an extraordinary feeling that filled me with hope. Perhaps feeling close to her will be the gift of my 44th year.

XXVII

Bucket List

THERE'S A RUMOR THAT THE TERM "bucket list" was created by the people behind the 2007 movie of the same name. The screenwriter claims it came out of his own list of things he wanted to accomplish before he died. He jotted down that list in the late 1990s and called it his "bucket list."

The movie, *The Bucket List*, rooted in the idiom "kick the bucket," certainly popularized the term, but we can't be sure that the writer was the first person to ever put those words together. It's great for him if so. I question the truth of its first use, partially because I am almost certain my mom said it to me. Whether the phrase was actually said is not what was so poignant.

It was early in 1998, and my mom was planning a solo trip to Europe. I had never heard of a woman traveling alone. Yes, I had already gone to France on my own a few times by then, but it was as an exchange student. Only my flights were solo. The rest of the time, I was living with a family. The idea of my mom gallivanting around Europe on her own for much of the trip was odd but inspiring. Now I adore solo travel.

Mom planned to go to France first with a French friend of ours from my school and our barn, and then she would stay with my host family in Paris for a little bit before heading out on her own to The Netherlands. That French woman was the same one who arrived in the waiting room the night Mom died and sat with me. I still don't know who called her to come to the hospital. I can't remember where else Mom went other than France and The Netherlands. I vividly remember her confidence every time I told her that it was odd for her to travel on her own. I guess it made sense for teenagers to explore without their parents, but it didn't make sense to me that a mother would go without her husband or kids. We were going to expand our world by becoming fluent in other languages and immersing ourselves in other cultures. Mom didn't know a full sentence in a language other than

English, but I remember being pleasantly surprised at how determined she was to do this for herself. She deserved to put herself first for once. Language barriers aside, she was always curious about other cultures and couldn't wait to be a tourist. She would tell me that she wanted to spend time really soaking in every art museum without her kids complaining. She was an artist, and she wanted to visit some of the world's greatest art museums at her own pace.

My memory is of her referring to this trip as her "bucket list trip," but, according to the writer of *The Bucket List*, she couldn't have used the term. Maybe she did. Maybe she didn't. It's what she meant, though, because each time she said it, I distinctly remember telling her, "Stop calling it that! Those are the things people do before they die." While we can't ever be certain about her calling it a "bucket list trip," I am positive about my reaction and can even remember having that chat in the game room of our Houston home that separated my room from my brother's.

Her response to my absolute horror that she would categorize her trip as stuff she wanted to do before she died was always the same. "Well, that's what this is. I want to make sure I do all these things before I die." What none of us knew was that she would die that year. Every time I think about her European trip in May 1998, I am comforted that she made it happen. She didn't let anything get in the way of this trip, and I love that for her. It was, and is, an inspiration.

Around that time, or perhaps a little before, she made a promise to my paternal great-aunt, paternal grandmother, and me. As always, the backstory is helpful. My grandmother, who my brother and I called "Beebaw," had polio when she was a toddler, and she had lifelong comorbidities as a result. The most minor of her issues was that she walked slowly. When she traveled internationally, it was almost exclusively attached to one of my grandfather's work trips, and it had been a long time since that was even possible. On our annual summer vacations to Rehoboth Beach, she couldn't go to the beach. It was too tough for her to walk on the sand, and my great-aunt would stay with her while we jumped waves in the cold Atlantic Ocean. My Papa did not enjoy doing much that was touristy on his work trips apart from touring cathedrals. Her health would limit how much she could do on her own while he worked on these trips.

Her sister, my great-aunt Peggy, lived abroad with a much more adventurous life but still unable to choose which countries she saw. Her husband was in the CIA during the Cold War, and they lived in West Africa and Eastern Europe. She regaled us with stories and lamented that she never truly knew everything her husband did as an agent. When they were back home in Maryland, a black car would regularly pull up outside of her house, and her husband would hop in. She would have no idea how long he'd be gone or where he was going. It was remarkable that she was able to relocate with him for those longer periods. One time, I was visiting her from college for a couple of days, and she was making me breakfast. "Every time I use this pan, I think about how often I made him breakfast, a car would pull up, he'd leave without saying much, and I'd toss his breakfast." Neither my grandmother nor my great-aunt ever felt like they got to fully experience countries like a normal tourist. Both shared with me a desire to see Ireland. I don't know why they chose Ireland or why it piqued their interest so much that they expressed such an enthusiastic desire to visit. I don't know why they shared it with me either, but I'm so glad that they did.

It isn't clear how the message got to my mom that Aunt Peggy and Beebaw wished to see Ireland. Maybe it was from me or directly from one of them, but more likely the former. I do know that it instantly excited my mom. She immediately had one of her creative and fun ideas. I get the same look on my face that she had when given the opportunity to plan something meaningful for someone. She declared that we would go on a girls' trip to Ireland and take Beebaw and Aunt Peggy. It took me a moment to realize she was serious.

Mom was thrilled at her own idea. I can still feel her excitement. My dad's family, particularly his parents and

Aunt Peggy, were true family to my mom. She felt loved by them in ways she hadn't by her own family. Going on a girls' trip with the family matriarchs would be a beautiful way to acknowledge that love, and it would be a lifelong memory for all four of us. She didn't have to tell me that explicitly, but I knew. She admired and respected Beebaw and Aunt Peggy and taught me to do the same.

As part of the trip, Mom suggested that she and I would ride horses in Ireland for a day or two. She noted that Bee-baw would need some time close to the hotel, and our two elderly relatives would be more than fine spending some quiet days while we cantered through fields. To her surprise, I was hesitant at the idea of riding at first. On my travels, my mom had always encouraged me to avoid activities and restaurants that were the same as they were at home. She pushed me to ensure all my experiences abroad were new and unique to wherever I was. Anytime I went to France, she'd remind me to speak French and avoid any American fast-food restaurants. "Soak up the culture," she'd say. I took that to heart and still do. I told her, "But we ride at home all the time." She enthusiastically explained that many equestrians aim to have riding holidays all over the world as a memorable way to travel and see unique places, and Ireland was a top destination. The idea of riding in Ireland made her even more excited, and, seeing her joy at having such a life-changing adventure with my favorite relatives and me, gave me hope. Thankfully, Aunt Peggy and Beebaw loved the idea, too. I was already daydreaming about a girls' trip with my favorite women in our family, and I knew it would be one memory after another.

Beebaw had a stroke. It was the summer before my senior year of high school, and we were going on a road trip to look at colleges. We had a French exchange student with us. She was the same age as me and from the family who invited me to their home for two summers in France, and it was her second time staying with us. On the road trip, we headed to Ohio first to see Beebaw and Papa after her stroke. She was still in a long-term care facility for rehabilitation. I had never seen her like that before. Despite all her health issues, nothing ever held her back. It was the first time I ever saw her appear frail. We were told she had not taken any steps with the walker or on her own yet, and it seemed that was a concern to her care team. I was surprised she had not pushed through and knocked down any physical obstacle on her way toward healing. Well, I was surprised and scared.

It's important to add here that my mom consistently instructed us to speak properly and respectfully to Beebaw and Papa, more so than to any other adults. Apparently, all of that went out the window the first day we visited her in rehab. I stood down the hallway, facing her. She was with her PT or OT caregiver with her hands on a walker and ready to practice walking. All these years later, I still don't know where the words came from, but I said, "Beebaw, I am not going to push you around Ireland in a wheelchair." Immediately, I regretted it. Everyone stared at me. I accepted that I'd probably be grounded when we got in the car. I couldn't even make eye contact with my mom after saying it. Beebaw and I were looking at each other like we were in a duel, and her therapist was wide-eyed at my comment. Her response was probably only seconds later, but it felt like an eternity. Beebaw said nothing. Instead, she gripped the walker tightly and took her first post-stroke steps. There was no way she was going to miss that trip to Ireland.

Unfortunately, we all missed the trip to Ireland. Beebaw needed a
wheelchair more than not, and her left arm had a life of its own after the stroke. She would joke that it would grab and throw things in the kitchen without her thinking about it. She also needed an at-home caregiver. None of that stopped her from being my beloved Beebaw. She later taught her caregiver how she hand-painted clothing on gingerbread men each year for me and sent enough to college for me to pass them out to every girl on my dorm floor. But Beebaw's health wasn't the only reason we never went on our girls' trip. Mom died that same year.

Mom got her bucket list trip the same year she died. She did it. No one knew she would die, but she fulfilled travel dreams anyway. I am grateful she did not let any excuse stop her. She put herself first for once, and it gave her unforgettable experiences. It made her year. Part of how I honor the uncertainty of having reached her age is doing the same.

I am fulfilling the dream. The trip that Beebaw, Aunt Peggy, Mom, and I dreamed about taking together is happening now. I am writing this chapter from the plane on the way to Dublin. Once there, I'll hop on a train at Heuston Station and head to Killarney where I will go on a five-day, six-night riding holiday along the Ring of Kerry. Like Mom's European art trip, my trip is intentionally solo. I've been referring to it as a "grief trip," and people's uncomfortable reactions have hovered between upsetting and entertaining. I imagine their expressions are similar to mine when Mom referred to her solo European trip as her "bucket list trip." With this holiday, I am celebrating the lives of Beebaw, Aunt Peggy, and Mom. I am honoring them and the trip we never got to take. I'm doing it for them. I'm doing it for me. It is my bucket list trip.

━━━━━━

XXVIII

Wheels Up

THANKS TO THE NOTORIOUSLY UNORGANIZED American Airlines, I nearly missed my connecting flight to Dublin. We left Houston late and landed in Chicago with minutes until boarding time. Given the flight was around 9 p.m., that was likely the last flight out. I ran through two terminals with an equestrian ringside backpack and a carry-on tote. My Adidas Sambas were raising blisters on my heels. While I was running, my phone rang. It was the airline asking if I was going to make it.

I wasn't the last one in line, nor was I the only one running to the gate from an earlier flight. The next leg was led by Aer Lingus, and their team was the exact opposite of American Airlines. The Irish fellow next to me helped stuff my ringside backpack in the overhead compartment. He noticed my riding helmet attached to the backpack, and that sparked a conversation. We chatted a bit, and then he got comfortable for a nap. To start switching my body to GMT, I opted to stay awake the whole flight, which isn't my norm. Given that all the riders in our group would have just one day to adjust to the time before we saddled up, I needed to do everything in my power to minimize jet lag. Unbeknownst to me, I was the sole rider who had more than an hour of time change to deal with as the rest of the group all hailed from Europe.

I took off my shoes and quickly put on slippers before grabbing my laptop out of my carry-on. When I was growing up, my mom always told me to take my shoes off on international flights. She said our feet swell, making our shoes too tight. I kept doing that ages after she died, but then one year I realized I was walking around the plane and into those teeny, bacteria-filled bathrooms in my socks, and that was when I started traveling with soft, packable slippers that can go in the wash when I get home. After following Mom's advice with a sanitary twist, I put my laptop on the tray table and opened the Word document that contained my manuscript in progress. My working title for this book was *The Day I Die*. By the time you read this, that may or may not be the title. Regardless, I noticed my seatmate peek at my computer, and his eyes widened. I opted to pretend not to notice and scroll to where I'd recently left off. Part of me wanted to tell him why I was going to Ireland. My riding helmet already led me to share it was a riding holiday, and he shared that his brother was a farrier in Australia. I waited for an opening — such as "Why did you decide to do this trip?" None came. I didn't push it. It reminded me of when Mom first died, and I wanted people to ask.

After Mom died, I expected and wanted everyone I bumped into, even if they were strangers, to know she died and ask me about it. I needed to talk about her and her death. As time went on, even people who knew her stopped saying her name, including family. Why were they so afraid to talk about her? As the countdown to Ireland began, I felt this same feeling creeping back. I wanted people to ask why I was going. When fellow riders would say what a dream the trip sounded like, I wished they'd ask why I decided to go, and I hoped my seatmate would do the same. Once we were all in the saddle on the first day, I expected the guides and fellow riders to ask everyone in the group why they were there. I wanted everyone to know. At the same time, there's a hesitation, because I don't want to be met with a sad face or pity. I wait, leave some crumbs, and hope someone will ask questions with curiosity and empathy.

In the months before the trip, people's reactions to my purpose for this trip were mixed. Some were excited and admitted some jealousy about the horse portion of the trip. As soon as I mentioned why, there would either be silence or a mumbled "How neat" or something similar. People were pretty bewildered by the idea of a grief trip. Maybe it was unusual. One day, however, I was on the phone with one of the women I was currently supporting in her grief over the death of her mom. She started talking about a trip, and she asked, "Is a grief trip a thing?" I never revealed that I was a motherless daughter like her or that I was about to embark on my own grief trip. I simply told her that it sounded like a healthy and healing idea and that others have taken similar trips. She felt validated.

My seatmate didn't ask about my book nor why I picked Ireland for this epic riding trip. He took his nap while I wrote and watched the fairly good selection of British and Irish TV and movies available on my seat's TV screen. I'm a bit obsessed with British TV.

Hours later, we were descending into Dublin just before noon on August 16. My eyes filled with tears that were quickly blinked away. I mouthed the words, "I did it, Mom. I'm here" as our wheels touched the runway. I couldn't stop staring out the tiny window until it was time for us to squeeze our way off the plane and through customs. Given my run through the Chicago airport, I was anxious as we watched the bags circle around the carousel. I had connected through Chicago twice in the past for international flights, and both times my luggage had been lost. Thankfully, my suitcase eventually arrived, and I released a breath I had been holding. As I made my way to the bus that would take me across town to Heuston Station for my train to Killarney, I had a feeling that I hadn't had since 1998. I felt like I was wearing a sign that said, "My mom is dead." This time, however, it didn't make me want a hug from anyone who was willing, nor was I on the verge of tears. I felt empowered by my grief.

⸻

XXIX

Literal Signs

WHILE ORGANIZING MY TRIP, I WAS INTEN-TIONAL about leaving time to explore Dublin before and after the riding holiday. It wouldn't be a lot, but it would give me a taste of life along the River Liffey. Before the riding holiday, I had just under two hours to push my luggage around in the vicinity of the train station, and the end of the trip gave me nearly six hours before my flight to London. I had to be smart and strategic about that time.

I'd researched pubs within a ten-minute walk of the station for lunch, and the long bus ride from the airport gave me great views of the city and helped me narrow my lunch choices further. I peeked inside the train station when the bus arrived to make sure I knew where to go and to double-check boarding time. I made my final decision on lunch and crossed the bridge over the River Liffey with my back-pack, carry-on bag, and wheeled suitcase. Immediately, I noticed a long line of people waiting to get into the pub I had chosen for lunch. There was another pub next door, and something caught my eye. The pub was called "Ryan's of Parkgate Street," and it was on my list already, but what surprised me was a metal sign that said, "F.X. Buckley," and had a cutout of a cow on it. I learned that F.X. Buckley is a group of steakhouses, but Buckley has a deeper meaning for me that added to my trip's grief focus. Buckley was the name of my Boston Terrier who died six months prior to my trip to Ireland.

The kindest Brazilian waitress guided my belongings and me to a seat and handed me a menu. The menu was full of "Buckley steak" items. My original plan was for my first meal on Irish soil to be fish and chips, which is already my go-to comfort meal, but I had to seal my grief trip with a Buckley steak sandwich and a Guinness. It felt as though I was being told, "You did the right thing coming here." My lunch was delicious and gave me indescribable comfort, and, after some waiting, I boarded a train to Killarney with a quick change in Mallow on the way.

Once the train arrived in Killarney, I made the twelve-minute walk to the McSweeney Arms Hotel to check in for the night. As soon as I was in my room, I went to the window to take in the view. Directly across the street was a pub called "Buckley's Pub." I couldn't believe it. It was clear where I'd be eating dinner. I even spotted his name at the Aran Islands sweater shop amongst the Irish clan names, and it was news to me that his name was so prevalent in Ireland. Seeing Buckley's name everywhere let me know I wasn't alone, and I was where I needed to be. It felt like the night before an Iron Man Triathlon, or so I imagined it would be. Mom loved to run, but I'm more of an apocalyptic runner. If I'm running, it's the end of the world, dinosaurs are back, or Jesus has returned. After dinner and shopping along Killarney's high street, I peered at the people in the pub beneath our rooms to see if any of them looked like equestrians and even asked the waitress if she knew who they were hoping to introduce myself. She wasn't sure, but she found my secret inquiry amusing. Instead, I ended up talking about the Garda and football with people at the bar over pints of Guinness. Any nerves that I had about the trip in general gave way to childlike excitement. The girls' trip officially started even though three of the four girls the trip was meant for died in 1998, 2002, and 2020. I was the only one alive, and I was making it happen for all of us.

XXX

Go Raibh Maith Agat

DURING DINNER AT BUCKLEY'S BAR, I asked the bartender whether the framed merchandise they had on the wall were for sale — they were, and I bought shirts for Patrick and me — and how to say "thank you" in Irish. We now proudly wear shirts with "Buckley's Bar: Killarney, Ireland" emblazoned on them. The bartender and two older gentlemen at the bar, who appeared to be regulars, had me repeating "Go raibh maith agat" until I had the pronunciation right. I told them there was no way I'd remember it.

The three men wondered why I wanted to learn that phrase in particular. There was an easy answer. "I think we should always learn how to say 'thank you' in the local language when we travel. It shows kindness, gratitude, and compassion." They loved my reasoning and lifted their pints in my direction while saying, "Sláinte!" in unison.

Not long after meeting the other riders in my group, I told them about my night wandering around Killarney and attempting to add "thank you" in Irish to my vocabulary. The group was made up of a German woman, a Dutch woman, an Irishman, and me. Our riding guides were French and Czech. My new friends asked me how to say my new phrase, as they recognized the importance. Our Irish buddy wanted to ensure I was saying it correctly. Predictably, I'd already forgotten. He helped us all say it, and throughout the week, he would nudge me at pubs when we were grabbing post-ride pints so that I would say "Go raibh maith agat" to bar staff as our pints were pulled. The bartenders beamed at me thanking them in their language. Centuries ago, there was an attempt to erase their language by the English, and there is a strong movement to keep it alive. My efforts to speak in a language that meant so much to them did not go unnoticed. As the days of the trip went on, it became the most powerful "thank you" I've ever said. My girls' trip — even without the other three intended attendees — was full of joy, grief, and connection, and it was indescribable.

Go raibh maith agat to every horse and human who healed parts of me I didn't realize still needed care, along the Ring of Kerry. The people and horses of Ireland reminded me that grief and gratitude coexist.

Go raibh maith agat, indeed.

XXXI

Present for Every Stride and Every Step

EACH RIDER BOOKED THROUGH A DIFFERENT equestrian vacation company or directly through Killarney Riding Stables. My travel agency was Active Riding Trips out of the United States, and they were phenomenal in the lead-up to the trip. They even enjoyed the videos from my helmet cam and photos I posted so much that they requested to use them. I proudly agreed. There was a limit of twelve riders, plus two guides, and we were lucky to have only four of us for our two guides to lead.

The trip itself was run by the staff at Killarney Riding Stables, and we were matched with horses based on our experience and preferences. Ed was assigned to me. He was a Connemara cross, who stood no more than 15.2 hands. The manager of the stables said he was "lively," and I asked her to elaborate. "This is my vacation," I reminded her while thinking about how my own thoroughbred could be described the same way. "Oh, he's forward. That's it." Perfect. I didn't want a kick ride, but I also didn't need to buck my way through the bogs. Ed turned out to be my ideal companion for the week.

Mom would've loved Ed except he wasn't very affectionate until I showed him massage techniques I'd learned from Gunner's bodyworker. Ed meets a lot of people and wasn't there to be best friends with every rider, but he had the time of his life on every ride. He knew exactly where we were each day. The moment I put my foot in the stirrup for the first time, he let me know that we were going to have fun as long as I allowed myself to connect with him. And I did.

What Mom would've loved about Ed is that he was a wonderful reminder of how horses can show us God and the world. He showed me how to have fun in the saddle again with zero pressure to be perfect or to impress anyone. Riders had to always stay behind the lead guide, and Ed had to be second. He couldn't contain his excitement and would get frustrated further back in the line of horses. Despite making this particular five-day trek regularly, he was thrilled every second of it. Ed let me know that I would not take a moment of our voyage around the Ring of Kerry for granted, because he wouldn't. It didn't matter how many times he'd toured a rider around this breathtaking part of Ireland. Ed loved every moment.

Our tour around the Ring of Kerry was an inn-to-inn ride, meaning that every day or two, we would bring our luggage with us in the morning, and it would be delivered to our next destination that we would ride to throughout the day. We stayed in pub hotels with decades' (or more) of history. Depending on the route for the day, we rode four to six hours per day with hour-long stops at some point for lunch and to give the horses some well-deserved rest. Our nights were spent in Killarney, Glenbeigh, and Waterville. Our days were spent in the saddle. We trotted along tight Irish roads, trail rode along ponds and through both bogs and a river, and we cantered up mountains and on beaches as the waves crept toward us. It was freedom like I'd never felt.

Our first and last nights were spent at the McSweeney Arms in Killarney, and there was a stark contrast in those nights. On August 16, none of us knew what the others looked like or anything about anyone else. Each one of us made different dinner plans and spent that evening in Killarney independently. On August 22, however, it was the opposite. We finished the ride that morning and napped or looked out the windows of our taxi van quietly on our way back to Killarney. We made dinner plans at a pub in town and went shopping for Irish sweaters together. Two of us stayed up for one last pint together in the McSweeney Arms' pub, and we had one final deep conversation about life, current events, and my 8,000 questions about Irish history were answered. While our first night was spent on our own, our last night felt like lifelong friends meeting up for good food and great conversation before we all headed home. We had such a profound experience together, regardless of what led us to view the Ring of Kerry through a horse's ears, and it's weeks like this one that change you forever. We all had unique and equally important reasons for taking the trip. Our conversations in the saddle were minimal as we were all in a line and taking in the view. We were giggling about sheep chasing us, warning each other about a bull in a pasture ahead, or pointing out where Luke Skywalker lived. Over meals and at the pubs, however, we chatted as if we'd known each other for our entire lives. Over pints, I was asked about my mom, and no one expressed pity. They demonstrated love and empathy.

Mom, my paternal grandmother, and my paternal great-aunt were with me every stride and step. Their presence was felt and impossible to ignore. There are certain activities, photos, and places that trigger the memory of someone we love who died. That is normal. We may think of someone when we bake their famous Christmas cookies, watch the World Series, or when another *Downton Abbey* movie is released. I'm lucky to have these memories. Depending on the moment, they can be comforting or trigger big grief emotions. Grief triggers are all part of the process, and they help me continue relationships with the people and pets I've lost. After 27 years without my mom, these experiences were more seldom. The same types of moments that connected me with Beebaw and Aunt Peggy were brief but still important. This trip was for them, and the connection to them was undeniable.

I could see Beebaw and Aunt Peggy sitting on a bench, beaming with their crooked-toothed smiles, and telling me stories about how they tormented each other as kids. I could see Mom overwhelmed with every bit of history we'd encounter on rides, such as monuments to the people killed in the Irish Civil War or ancient homes from centuries ago. The last places they lived were Avon Lake, OH, Derwood, MD, and Houston, TX. None of them had ever set foot in Ireland. But they were there. I didn't feel
alone anymore. I could feel them every stride and every step.

———

XXXII

Voices Carry

O NE OF THE FIRST TEXTS I SENT my dearest friend after only a few hours in Ireland was "Every portrayal of Ireland and Irish people in movies and TV is accurate." And I meant that as a compliment. They were the kindest and most welcoming people I'd ever met, and I had traveled all over Western Europe, the Middle East, Mexico, and Australia in the past. Both Dublin and the small towns we visited were full of idyllic, colorful buildings, and the countryside was a shade of green that I didn't know existed outside of a Boden clothing ad. The history of Ireland drew me in, which often happens to me when I travel. I wanted to soak in everything in front of me and discover what was beneath the surface. Everywhere I turned, there was something I knew my mom, Beebaw, and Aunt Peggy would have loved if we had been able to have our special girls' trip.

Every room I stayed in had its own electric kettle, teacups, and bags of Barry's Irish breakfast tea. I drink Yorkshire Gold every morning at home, which is one of England's number one teas, and Barry's hit the spot for me for my morning cuppa. All three of those wonderful ladies would've loved that. I brewed a cuppa each morning as I read my Bible app on my phone and put on the day's riding outfit. Many of the breakfast options, especially toast with incredible jams and perfectly cooked eggs, felt like Aunt Peggy was cooking for me with her decades-old cast iron skillet. When I was in London in late 2019 into early 2020, I picked up a couple of jars of jam at Borough Market and mailed them to Aunt Peggy in Maryland once I returned to Texas. A couple of months later, against my advice, she was moved to a nursing facility.

She had previously told me that I was the only one that let her talk about dying. She said, "You never change the subject. Your dad and everyone else can't handle it." I could handle it. She told me she would die quickly if anyone put her in a home. I told my dad and uncle. They minimized my input. My voice being dismissed is all too common in my family. Aunt Peggy died less than two weeks after she was admitted to the nursing home. It was March 2020, and, after 96 years of blazing a trail wherever she went, no one was able to be at her burial due to COVID-19. I found some comfort when I learned that she insisted the jam I bought her in England go with her to the nursing facility. She had treasures from all over the world in her home, but she would not let those jams I bought her be left behind. Every morning in Ireland, I smiled at the basket full of delicious jams on the breakfast table that put all American jams to shame.

My paternal grandmother was known for her kindness, gentleness, generosity, and ability to make every person feel loved, either through her smile, her baked goods, or her small yet big ways of caring for others. I was only in Ireland one night before I knew how easily she would fit in. Both Ireland and England are full of people who have a natural way of making everyone they meet feel like they have known them their whole lives, just like my Beebaw. Everyone Beebaw met felt like they were her family. She saved my mom and loved her in a way my mom's own mother never could. Scratch that. She loved my mom in a way her own mother never wanted to. Despite a history of being verbally, and probably physically, abused by her stepfather and, at a minimum, neglected by her mother, my mom led with her heart.

That was either her nature that couldn't be stiffened by her family, Beebaw's influence, or a combination.

I may have mentioned elsewhere that I couldn't remember what my mom's voice or laugh sounded like anymore. In fact, those sounds were gone within months of her death. When someone dies now, we have countless videos on our phones and social media of them. When my mom died, it was a chore to get out the family camcorder, and we only used it to record us riding. Our voices still weren't heard on those. The last recording we had of Mom's voice was on our family's answering machine. Those aren't even a thing now. When my brother was home from college, he deleted Mom's voice on the answering machine. My dad and I were livid. We loved calling the house and hearing her. My brother, on the other hand, struggled with having her voice greet him when he called us when we weren't home. Dad's and my grief needed her "Please leave a message after the beep" speech. Nate's grief needed to not hear it. Not long after the answering machine tape was erased, I realized I couldn't remember what she sounded like. That all changed on August 18, 2025, in Glenbeigh, Ireland.

Decades after her death, our group walked and trotted through a small town and down a huge hill to reach Rossbeigh Beach near the village of Glenbeigh, where we were staying. Rossbeigh Beach is long and sandy, and it's on a peninsula that stretches into Dingle Bay, leading into the

North Atlantic Ocean. I was nervous about cantering in such an open area with waves on one side and sand dunes on the other, but I was ready. When the guides yelled, "Hup, hup!" as they always did to signal it was time for the group to canter, I felt the light rain in my face and gave Ed leg to let him know he could fly. What came next was inexplicable. I heard laughter. It wasn't from the guide in front of me or from the rider behind me. It was next to me. But no one was next to me. Tears began to flow from my eyes, and I smiled so big there was a legitimate concern that I'd get rain or sand in my mouth. There was no doubt in my mind whose laughter it was. It was my mom's.

Call me crazy. I don't care. I hadn't heard that laugh in decades, but I instantly knew it was hers. I laughed through my tears, and I was grateful for the rain that blended with my tears to avoid anyone asking why I was crying. I was fulfilling a dream for both of us and cantering in the Irish rain down a beach. She was with me. She was loving it. She was laughing.

For the first time in a long time, I knew she was with me in a very real way. "You're here," I said to myself. "We're flying together, Mom." If I'd let Ed go as much as he wanted, he probably would've literally flown. I learned later that he gets a little excited on beach rides, but the guides said I handled him well. On the technical side, I had soft hands with a tickle on the reins every so often while avoiding what he hated, which was getting heavy in his mouth. He responded well to my legs and seat, and we were connected. He gave me freedom, and I knew we weren't riding alone. Yes, there were two guides and some other riders, but Mom was with us, too. When I ride at home, I always feel connected with Mom and God, but this was different. I felt this in my body, not only in my soul.

I cried. I laughed. I never felt so free in my life.

XXXIII

A Community in North London

AFTER MY WEEK IN IRELAND, I headed to London for a few days. Every time you travel, you should feel a little different. We can't possibly be the same after immersing ourselves in another country's culture, history, and language, nor should we be.

London has done a number on me. The first time I was there was with my family in 1990, and there's a great candid photo of Mom, Nate, and me sitting on the steps of the National Gallery. I went again in 1998, days before Mom's neurosurgery. While studying abroad in Paris, a few friends from Sweet Briar College and I also met up in London, and then I went as a guest of the Premier League and Arsenal Football Club in 2019 into 2020. While I have undeniably spent more time in France than England, there is a strange, peaceful, and spiritual feeling that comes over me when I wander the streets of London. It feels like it was meant to be my home, and I feel safe, free, curious, and comfortable amongst the millions of people speaking different languages, the Roman streets, reminders of royal lineage and history, and the Thames. I feel like myself.

I picked up a soccer ball — football — a few years before my parents let me take my first riding lesson. When I was 4, my dad put a Pelé VHS tape in my Easter basket. It was a struggle to find football on TV in the United States when I was growing up, but we did have the World Cup. I loved every second, and it was the one time that Nate and I were guaranteed to enjoy each other's company. Every four years, we were friends for a few weeks. In the late 1990s while I was attending an international school, I would hear people talking about their favorite club. At that point, I mostly followed football on the international level. Most of the time, my classmates' favorite club was from their home country. I wanted one, too. Initially, I figured it would have to be Paris Saint-Germain (PSG) because of my summers as an exchange student in Paris (and because I purchased one of their kits during the summer in Paris), but that didn't feel right. I wanted a Premier League club to follow. After some research, I started to find myself in north London. Arsenal's manager and star player were both French. I'm certainly not the only Gooner (name for Arsenal supporters) who was drawn to the club because of Arsène Wenger or Thierry Henry, but there was something else about Arsenal that drew me in. Their French leaders simply solidified it. I couldn't name it, but I knew Arsenal was the club for me. In 2000, when I was studying at the Sorbonne, I read *Fever Pitch* by Arsenal supporter Nick Hornby while traveling to class on the Métro in Paris, and the book validated my connection to Arsenal. It gave words for my draw to the Club, just like grief books had given me words to describe, validate, and articulate my feelings. *Fever Pitch* confirmed that I was right. I went from a casual fan to a full supporter. Arsenal was home, and from then on, I was hooked. As the Premier League grew in the US, I started scheduling meetings and horse rides around matches. I made up for lost time of not having access to regular matches by never missing one, having special Arsenal pajamas that I had to wear the night before a match, and a special mug that I had to have my morning Yorkshire Gold in on match day.

In nearly 20 years of fandom and numerous trips to London, I had yet to see them play in person. In 2019, we packed up the four dogs and drove to Charlotte, NC and later Washington, D.C. to see Arsenal on their summer US tour. The first person I saw on the pitch was Stuart MacFarlane, Arsenal's photographer, and I freaked out. Fast forward six years later, and I named a dog after him. As the players came out to warm up, tears began to flow. My fiancé captured that moment, and I later posted it for my handful of followers on Twitter. What followed wasn't expected. Arsenal, some of the club's players, and about 2 million people, watched the video of me crying. A couple of months later, I was told on live TV that Arsenal and the Premier League were hosting me for a match, which turned out to be two matches.

I took a friend with me who turned out to be the opposite of who I thought she was. She was yet another person to take advantage of a person who was constantly desperate for companionship and hurt them. She got a free trip to London, and she gave me pain in return. But London didn't hurt me. Arsenal didn't hurt me. In fact, as I gathered with 60,000 of my friends at Emirates Stadium, I learned a new definition of community.

Growing up in church and as a rider, I knew what community felt like, but people in the church are really good about showing others how human they are in a bad way. Arsenal F.C. was what the Church claimed to be. While my Christian faith remains strong, I feel closer to God with horses and more in community in London's N5.

Football is called "the beautiful game," and it unites people around the world. Since I was young, I've been drawn to the sport itself but also to people from other countries. I wanted to get to know them, their stories, and their countries. Even looking back to when I was discerning which club was best for me, I was seeking to belong and was using the world's favorite sport as a means to do so. Good thing I already loved the sport.

Apart from a few misogynistic comments on Twitter, everyone who identified as a part of Arsenal, whether as a fan, a steward, a journalist, a player, or the media team, made me feel at home. Back home in the US, anytime I see anyone in any Premier League shirt, I want to strike up a conversation and have a bit of banter. The bond is obviously stronger when they're decked out in our beautiful red and white.

When picking the dates for my trip to Ireland, I intentionally sought dates near the start of the Premier League season. It would be ridiculous to be only an hour flight from London and not be able to see my club, and August made sense for a couple of reasons. First, it was before Ireland's rainy season, and second, once the Premier League season begins, fixtures (matches) can be moved because of tournaments, international friendlies, or TV. Matches at the start of the season wouldn't be affected. Once the first home match was announced, I started the heavy task of trying to find a ticket, which is not easy. There are extensive waitlists for tickets. I got lucky, however, and was offered to purchase one from a fellow healthcare worker in the US. Her grandfather left his season ticket to his family in his will, and she managed them. No one in her family was going to use it that day, and all I had to do was transfer her the funds, and the ticket would be mine. The seats were amazing, and I loved that I was sitting in the seat of a man who wanted those cherished tickets to stay in his family after his death. His wishes weren't unusual. Many people leave their season tickets in their wills, but it felt like yet another bit of comfort for this griever. Ending my grief trip by sitting in the seat of a man who was loved and missed by both his family and the Arsenal family felt perfect.

On this trip, the Arsenal community proved itself to be my family yet again. I hung out with people I'd met on Twitter and with whom we share *Seinfeld* memes, darted around London to stock up on tea from Whittard's and Fortnum & Mason, and an Arsenal buddy, whom I have yet to meet, set up a private stable tour in Newmarket for me. I chatted with strangers over pints before the match, and the people sitting near me acted as if we'd been friends and seatmates for years. Arsenal made me feel like I belonged. I didn't feel alone. Being surrounded by all those people wearing red and white, singing together, and sipping pints of lager, made me feel like I was a part of something. That's big for a griever who has felt abandoned and alone for 27 years.

As the match started, we sang "The Angel (North London) Forever." I was used to singing it from my living room with the TV, and I was tearful as I was able to sing it in the stadium. I was overwhelmed with the sound of our whole community of 60,000 singing in unison.

We are forever connected thanks to our love for a team with a deep history and a strong presence, both globally and locally. Our love for the person we lost will never leave us if we wear our grief proudly like a football scarf. I cope with my loss with faith, animals, and the diverse, passionate, loving people who call Arsenal home.

———

XXXIV

Another Community, Another Club

I'VE SAID BEFORE THAT I JOINED A CLUB when Mom died that I never wanted to be a part of, and it's called Motherless Daughters. I use the term quite a lot, and, as far as I'm aware, it was coined by author Hope Edelman in her book by the same name. For years, regardless of where I was traveling both domestically and internationally, I always made sure that I had my Bible and *Motherless Daughters*. That probably changed somewhere between five and ten years after Mom's death, and now I only bring a travel-sized Bible for domestic travel and use a Bible app for international travel because I'm already at risk of my suitcase being too heavy and need space for infinite purchases.

I have always craved community, and I've been part of faith communities, barn communities, the global community of Arsenal fans, and chaplains. Each has given me space to be myself, grow, and connect with people with a similar interest. Some of those communities have also added significant emotional and spiritual pain to my life. I won't elaborate because that could be another book or Substack articles, but I can say that Arsenal F.C. and its supporters have always made me feel at home and as though I belong. That's what a community should be.

Motherless Daughters was given to me just weeks after Mom died, and I've recommended it dozens of times since then as a chaplain and as a bereaved daughter. Girls and women whose mothers died at a young age have an instant bond. Our collective trauma and grief changed us forever, and many of us have had similar experiences in the years after our mothers died. Since COVID-19, the book's author started weekly Zoom calls for motherless daughters in addition to her retreats and other programs. I knew about these calls and regularly clicked on the links she posted about them. I'd think about joining but would hesitate.

I told myself that joining the Motherless Daughters community wasn't a good idea for a handful of reasons. First, I said I couldn't justify any extra expenses as a chaplain with a horse, but when I really thought about it, the monthly cost was basically the same as a fajita dinner for two but with a much longer impact. Another obstacle I created was that I thought my loss was too long ago. All day, I tell people that we live with grief our whole lives, and I aim to be just one person who ensures a bereaved person doesn't feel judged by how long they are feeling the immense weight and pain of grief. And then I judge myself.

The last reason I gave myself not to join the Motherless Daughters community Zoom calls is rooted in my job. Years ago, a pastor told me, "It takes 5 years to get the seminary out of you." He was attempting to normalize how hard it is for a fresh seminary graduate to sit through someone's sermon without critiquing the structure, the illustrations, and every other aspect of the sermon. After a while, seminary graduates are once again able to be a participant like everyone else in the pew. That's the hope, anyway. I am highly critical of sermons when they're addressing hope, grief, and suffering, but that isn't because of my degree. It's because of my role walking alongside people who are dealing with pain. That pastor's advice led to one of my excuses for not joining the Motherless Daughters calls.

Like many chaplains, I struggle being a participant in church. There is such comfort in being part of a church, but it seems that the moment my vocation is discovered, I'm no longer permitted to learn and grow like everyone else. We need to be fed, too, especially if we're going to pour out to others all week in the deepest ways. It seems impossible, though. I can hide in a pew, but if I try to join a small group, I'm suddenly everyone's safe space. They are seeking advice and sharing their stories. I'm honored to be trusted, but I attempted to be a part of those communities for the same reasons they did and to have a moment where I didn't have to be a chaplain. I was concerned the same thing would happen on the Zoom calls. I was worried that it would be hard to be a participant, and I also worried I would be judged. Shame crept in. Would the other motherless daughters think I'm not good at my job if I am there for the same support they are seeking? I asked myself that question every time I considered being a part of the group.

In October of the year grief math was coming to a terrible end, I attended a free Zoom with Dr. Mary-Frances O'Connor, the author of *The Grieving Brain*, that Hope Edelman led. I loved the interview and the discussion in the chat was fruitful and safe. I found a community, and I wasn't going to let any of my real or perceived obstacles get in the way. I joined the monthly calls seconds after the chat with Mary-Frances concluded, and a couple of days later I was attending my first one. For the first month, I signed up for both the Tuesday evening and Thursday afternoon calls. I wanted to make sure I attended and didn't rely on the recordings of the calls, because I already have access to a wealth of grief articles and webinars for work. I didn't want to treat this the same way. The point of this was gathering with fellow motherless daughters as a community, and I figured that seeing how both of those different times of day felt for my energy and schedule would be helpful. I eventually decided the Thursday group was more my vibe because the time slot allowed for international motherless daughters to attend, and my emotional energy is typically at a good spot in the afternoon.

This was the support I needed when I was 17 and so alone, but I believe this was the exact season I needed to be around these women. My first session was two months before Mom's death anniversary when I'm the dreaded age of 44. As I buckled down to write my book, I heard the voices of women from all over the United States, England, and Western Europe, and their stories were validating. I wasn't alone.

Much to my pleasant surprise, I never had the urge to chaplain anyone. I listened to women share about their mothers and the long-term effects of early grief on their lives and felt like a participant. Under the faces of the motherless daughters, their names were not simply their first and last name. They also stated, "___'s daughter" and filled in the blank with their mom's name. I couldn't remember the last time that anyone referred to me as "Deb's daughter." It was incredibly heartwarming to see all these women proudly claiming whose daughter they were no matter how long it had been since they'd been able to hug or speak to their mothers.

I had not heard discussions like this before. Despite years of studying grief, being a supportive presence as brain-dead children are extubated, guiding a kid in accepting and processing that his cancer is terminal, and advocating for parents as they make major medical decisions for tracheotomies or chemotherapy, the stories these women shared were new to me as a chaplain. Their stories, however, were not new to me as a motherless daughter. Women nodded as a woman would share her fears or worries about her mom's upcoming death anniversary. Nearly every comment in the chat box had replies to it as women related to each other's experiences and shared deeply personal stories. They resonated with my comments on grief math and shared they did the same math. The number of women who had strained or frustrating relationships with their fathers was both shocking and validating. It wasn't just me. Bereaved fathers and motherless daughters were evidently a complex combination.

The Motherless Daughters Zoom calls felt similar to entering the grounds at the Emirates Stadium as clouds of fans in red and white gathered to cheer on Arsenal. I was at home with these women. It is a community rooted in grief, pain, and hope. None of us asked to join this club with a lifetime membership, but we were proud to be in it together and be what each other needed. We have automatic empathy and compassion for each other, and that builds trust and safety that is hard to come by.

XXXV

44 Years, 9 Months, and 6 Days

TODAY HAD BEEN LOOMING FOR YEARS yet inescapable since my 43rd birthday. Last year, when I turned 43, I could look forward to my next birthday like I was looking at it in a two-way mirror. I could see it, but it could not see me. On my 44th birthday, I could feel that same sense of dread I feel as each December 12 approaches. Each day since then felt as though it was leading up to my last. 9 months and 6 days from that birthday, I would die. People continue to tell me that I'm "just like [your] mother." If I am, then I'll die at the same exact age to the day that she did.

I woke up today and posted the quote above on the Instagram I run to validate and explore people's grief, let Stewie out to potty after his breakfast, and then got back in bed to cuddle him some more. I took vacation days for today and tomorrow, because there's no way I can provide the compassionate grief support people deserve today and tomorrow. I took off work these two days for me, honestly. In the past, I didn't work on December 12 for both the patients and me, but to push myself to submit the PTO request, I convinced myself it was only for the patients. I tend to feel guilty doing things for myself, but that's changed. Early in my grief journey, I told myself that "grieving isn't selfish." I was always so concerned about how other people were feeling, that I had to repeat that to myself for permission to grieve.

Experiencing feelings of fear, anxiety, sadness, and uncertainty about turning the age your parent was when they died is normal, and it has been quietly comforting to learn that countless others have felt the same apprehension approaching this milestone. I wonder if tomorrow will bring a sense of freedom, or dread, or nothing at all. I can imagine the freedom more easily than I can imagine the dread. Maybe that means something.

Every December, the 12th jumps out on the calendar. There's a cloud over it. From December 1–12, I replay those last conversations, moments, and decisions. I wish we could skip right to the 13th. Sometimes the 12th is as intense as predicted, and sometimes the days leading up to it are worse. Regardless, I often feel free on the 13th. I feel like a runner breaking through the finish line tape, and I think "I made it!" as if living another year without my mom is an accomplishment. In a way, it is. I'm surviving. Today, it seems as though there's an impassable wall between December 2 and December 3. I need to break through it like the Kool-Aid Man in order to live longer than my mom. That's daunting. Maybe that's the freedom washing over me.

With each Black Friday and Cyber Week email that popped in my inbox today, I thought, "Don't they know what today is?" in the same way that I used to wonder how dare someone bother me with mundane things immediately after the deaths of my mom and dogs. As I drove from my house to the barn, I had this feeling that everyone on the road could tell that my life could end today. It was just like the first few weeks after Mom died when I walked around with an imaginary sign (that didn't seem imaginary) on my forehead that said, "My mom is dead." It was honestly good that the farrier hadn't made it out to the barn to put on a shoe Gunner had thrown off in a one-man party in his pasture a few days ago. The temperature had dropped over 20 degrees, and that was a recipe for him to be a wild boy. If you already feel like you may not live through the day, then tempting fate by hopping on a spirited thoroughbred in the cold is not a good idea. Instead, I hand walked with him and smiled as he grazed. His bodyworker came, and we both love her sessions. She is so gifted, and I love that she sees us. I didn't realize how much peace it would bring both of us to have his appointment scheduled for today. The 90 minutes we spent with her was the only time I didn't reflect on being 44 years, 9 months, and 6 days old. The rest of the day, it was at the forefront of my mind and often manifested in sudden bursts of tears and tightness in my chest.

Parents almost always seem old to their kids, and I was no exception. I was aware that my mom died young, but she still didn't seem young to me. The hundreds of deaths for which I have been present as a chaplain were mostly infants and children, and the majority of the families I support now have lost someone in their 90s. Because of my work experience, anytime someone tells me that my mom died young, I agree but think, "She wasn't that young" as my mind flashes to the countless times I held parents' hands as life support was withdrawn from their toddlers after a traumatic drowning. My age when Mom died, coupled with my vocation, skewed my understanding of exactly how young my mom was at the time of her death. My opinion has definitely changed.

I am utterly shocked at how young I feel at 44 years old. While the uncertainty of living longer than Mom hangs over me, it is clear just how young Mom was. The children and newborns whose deaths I was present for were undoubtedly

way too young to lose their lives, and I'm giving myself permission to admit that Mom was, too. I don't feel old. Like
my mom was, I'm very active and constantly finding new,
inventive ways to occupy my time. She rediscovered her
love for art in the last couple of years of her life, and I've
done the same with writing. Emotionally, I feel defeated
and heavy with the idea of outliving her. Physically, I am
young, vibrant, and ready for more adventures at 44 and
beyond. Spiritually, however, I am somewhere in between
but safe regardless.

She was so young.

XXXVI

On the 7th Day

MERE MINUTES AFTER MIDNIGHT, I began to sob as if someone had removed the weight of a Clydesdale from my shoulders. I was officially older than my mom. I have always wondered if this day would come. For years, I couldn't imagine living past the age she died. All year, I was certain this was the year I'd die just as she did. It turns out, I was wrong, and it's not clear if that should feel like a cause for celebration or not. It's the final grief math equation.

Surprisingly, I felt free today. It was a strange feeling, and I was unusually relaxed the entire day as if nothing could alter my mood, even 6 bucks chasing a single doe in the arena while I tried to ride Gunner. It was as if I was released by something that had been hanging over me, but the knowledge that I'd outlived my mother was as full of uncertainty as attempting to navigate life without her since I was 17.

Alex Michaelides, the author of *The Silent Patient*, must have some experience with early loss or grief math. One of the protagonists of the book, Alicia Berenson, mentioned turning 33 and outliving her mother, who died at 32. I was in the midst of writing this book while simultaneously reading *The Silent Patient*, and I quickly hit "pause" and backed up my audiobook to hear the passage again. The character processed how disorienting and unnatural it felt to be older than her mom and continue to get older. Thankfully, that was the only way I connected to that unique character, but it was powerful to hear grief math depicted so well in a novel. As I read this section — well, as it was read to me on my library-loaned audiobook — I felt her words deeply. Mom stopped aging. I will continue to age.

My mom is younger than me. Imagine that. Imagine you are older than your parents while still being young yourself. It simply doesn't compute, but it's the reality for those of us who lost a parent young and live past the age they died. It is incredibly disorienting, yet here I am. Mom is forever

44 years, 9 months, and 6 days. She is stuck at the age she died, and I'm navigating a life she never knew.

She has missed watching her children grow, learn, make mistakes, and rise from each hurdle they faced. She's missed being a grandmother, something she dreamed about openly. While the world constantly changed, she is frozen at a time when dial-up internet was just beginning. I cannot imagine having to teach her to use an iPhone. AOL email was tough enough.

Both of Debra Shannon's children are now older than she ever was. I don't know if that milestone is as significant for a son whose mother died as it is to a daughter whose mother died, but I do know that being older than Mom has a feeling that no other age carries. Things are forever different. The before and after of her death is emphasized for me even now.

———————————

XXXVII

December 12, 2025

LAST WEEK AFTER OUTLIVING MOM, I rewrote my goals for the last chapters of this book. I scrapped plans to write about experiencing Mom Day at 44 years old. Waking up today changed that immediately. It's December 12, 2025.

Yesterday during the weekly Motherless Daughters call that I'm a part of, I was sharing how I felt about the 27th anniversary approaching and my plans for the day. I reported feeling better than in previous years. Outliving her seemed to remove the cloud that hangs over this day. Hours later, I burst into tears while binging a show on BritBox and said, "My mom is dead" to no one. Well, not no one. I thought I was recording a Marco Polo video message to my dearest friend, but I never hit record. Every year, the heaviness of her death hits me, and I reach a point where I need to say the facts out loud as if to wake me up to reality. She's dead.

I didn't take a vacation day from work today, because I took two days off last week for the days I turned her age at death and the day I outlived her. It's the first time in memory that I stayed scheduled to work the full day on December 12. To make up for it, I worked all week as if I were preparing for multiple vacation days. Over the last couple of years, I've not been serving as a pediatric chaplain, but it still feels like part of my identity and informs the care I give now. I'm providing grief support for families through a hospice, including adults and children, and I check on people multiple times for the first year after their loss. This week, I did all I could to limit the number of calls needed to make on the 12th. Front-loading my week with extra grief calls exhausted me emotionally but would be worth it. I slept in, and at 8:45 a.m. I was woken up by a phone call from a social worker. I immediately regretted not taking the day off. Throughout the conversation, I faked being cheerful and fully present for others, as I've done so many other times as a chaplain while feeling broken inside. The call was fine, but it seemed ominous for the rest of the day.

I discovered a handful of missed texts after ending the call with the hospice social worker. There were some from my dad in the group text with my brother and me. I said a little but not much given that his wife was mentioned in his text about all that has happened in 27 years. I know he didn't mean anything, but I only want to hear about my mom today. He knows her best, and he holds all the stories. He told a story from high school that didn't have anything to do with our mom but rather Vietnam, and now that I reflect on the text thread, not much of the lengthy text thread was actually about her. I wanted so much more from those texts. When I saw the first one that began, "27 years..." there was a glimmer of hope that I was about to read something reminiscent of the emails we used to receive many years ago, but it was quickly clear that wouldn't be the case. Nate never said a word all day. I've learned to have minimal expectations but still maintain hope that one day per year we can all speak vulnerably and honestly about her, engage in some healing storytelling, and express some emotions. I remain disappointed.

I also had some missed texts from my mom's closest sister. Mom adored this particular sister. For the first time in 27 years, my aunt expressed some love on this day. She told stories about my mom as a teenager, and she painted a vivid picture of her sitting on her bed in their shared room and being silly. I smiled. My aunt talked about my mom's handwriting, and I instantly remembered how everyone commented on her perfect handwriting. It looked like she used a ruler to guide her beautiful cursive. My own writing looks like I'm writing with the wrong hand. My aunt stated that, in the weeks after Mom's death, she collected all the letters Mom had written her and sent them to my dad to support him in his grief. My mom loved to write and mail letters to people. She would hand-write letters to me when I was in France, and I found some of them not too long ago. My aunt said the letters were full of my mom's joy for her life. I loved that. I loved that my aunt sent her treasured letters to my dad to help him grieve. It made me happy that someone cared for him like that, but it also confused me. She was the one I most expected to reach out and mother me when Mom died. I kept waiting for her to call and check on me, especially once I went to college only a few hours from her. She supported my dad. Now, all these years later, it confirms to me that adults simply don't know how to support a grieving child. They abandon us.

I'm thankful so many people cared for my dad. He had work friends, friends from high school, Pittsburgh friends, neighbors, and others. The adults who loved on me were either from the barn or my high school. My church never reached out. My family said nothing. I'm glad my aunt thought to send her letters to my dad to give him a window into the thoughts my mom shared with her closest sister while, at the same time, I wish those letters had been sent to me or, at a minimum, shared with me so that I could learn more about my mom from her own words.

The rest of the day looked similar to past Mom Days. I spent time at the barn. I don't feel as emotionally safe at this barn as I have at past ones for a host of reasons, which made me act like it was a normal day anytime others were nearby, but whenever Gunner and I were on our own I spoke to him on the verge of tears. In the past, I felt safe enough to share with a few people at the barn what the day was, and they were always kind and compassionate. I kept silent about the significance of the day at the barn today for the first time. Later, Stewie and I went to a local brewery that has a huge area to explore. Every time I was in the car, I cried while listening to The Cure on shuffle. It's quite possible that I'm the only person to fully sob while singing to "Friday, I'm in Love." I felt transported to car rides where Mom and I would sing that together, and memories came flooding back of her telling Nate and me to name a daughter Elise after the song "A Letter to Elise" played.

My dogs and horse make me feel safe to be human when so many others communicate the opposite. Because of that, they are by my side as much of every December 12 as possible, and this year was no exception. I also aim to be outside as much as possible where I feel peaceful and free. In the evening, Stewie and his parents took him to see Christmas lights, and the night ended with a toast to my mom. Tears flowed intermittently and heavily throughout the day. This year felt the same as other years in a familiar way, but it was also noticeably different because of the grief math.

Death anniversaries are, in themselves, grief math. Each year I think to myself, "This is the last day she lived." The next day, a new cycle of grief math begins, but 2025 had a twist. In her lifetime, she saw December 13–31, the months of January and February, and March 1–5 only 43 times. She was 44 from March 6–December 12. That's it. Her last day of life was December 12, and she was 44. Today is the last day we shared. From now on, every day I greet is a day she never saw.

<hr>

XXXVIII

What's Next?

DECEMBER 13 FELT DIFFERENT. December 13, 1998 was the first full day my mom was dead. I was in a daze. We all were. That same day in 1999–2024 felt as though all the grief math problems were erased or expanded. December 13, 2025 felt foreign. I am 44, and, for the rest of my life, I am navigating days my mom never saw. She never woke up on December 13 at 44 years old. She never celebrated Christmas at 44 or rang in the new year at that age.

In two months, I will be 45 years old. It's the first age I'll reach that Mom never saw. It is full of uncertainty. When a parent dies young, such as my mother at 44, then being older than that can feel as though you're living in the unknown. There is no parental guide on how to live at that age or what that age looks like. There is no blueprint on aging. There is no one to tell you at what age their hair went grey or to offer wisdom on navigating life at that age and later. 45 is uncharted territory for me, and a lot of adult children have faced the grief math of living longer than their deceased parent. The unknown is scary.

I have so many questions that I'd ask her about aging, but she never received the gift of getting older. We often forget that it is a gift to age, because we spend so much time and money to reverse it. If you've experienced death, either personally or through work in healthcare, funeral work, law enforcement, or the military, then you are well aware of how lucky we are to age.

My mom would be 71 now, but instead, she's forever 44. She's missed 27 years of birthdays, Christmases, Easters, Thanksgivings, Mother's Days, graduations, horse shows, riding lessons, and cantering through Ireland's bogs and beaches. She missed meeting people and animals who have made my life better. While she's missed being present for those milestones, celebrations, and relationships, her absence from each of those has been palpable.

I assumed the last grief math problem would be on the day I outlived her, but it appears there's another one. For the rest of my life, I will be able to do subtraction rather than addition. My calculation will be my age minus 44, which equals how many years I lived longer than my mother. As of now, I've only lived days longer than her, but by the end of February, the answer will be 1. I wonder if grief math will restart in my mind, or if I'll have peace over it and chuck it aside like I did school math. It has been my constant companion as so many people have come and gone from my life. It has been my guide and connected me to the profound loss of my mom.

Grief math is much more significant to me, and many grievers, than getting an "A" in algebra (which I did not do). I do know that grief math is common. Before beginning this book, I posted some questions on my social media accounts about grief math. A few people responded, each sharing detailed grief math they had done and complex feelings as they approached the day their parent died. Interestingly, everyone who responded had lost the same-gender parent. In the Motherless Daughters Community, grief math is frequently mentioned directly or indirectly. My experiences were validated. For once, I didn't feel alone. Grief math connects all the dots of our loss.

My prayer is that grief math is as healing and comforting to other grievers as it has been to me. Writing the book I wanted to read has been an even greater gift than I anticipated. It was emotional, draining, and required me to courageously share vulnerable stories, and I am thankful for the hard writing days that required my best loose-leaf tea to recover.

Grief is hardly how we are told it will be. We don't go from denial to bargaining to anger to sadness to acceptance and move on. It's more like a tumbleweed yet also hits us like waves. The similes and metaphors for grief are endless but nevertheless powerful. We can set ourselves up for failure if we assume there will be an end date on grief. The condolence cards and casseroles will stop coming. Friends and co-workers will stop asking how you are. There will be days when you laugh again. Give yourself a lot of grace. Erase the idea of a cycle, stages of grief, or a timeline. Let grief, and all the complex emotions of grief, flow. A day will arrive when you can celebrate their life while remembering them. If adding up the days, months, and years your beloved pets and people have been gone or how old they'd be gives you hope and helps make sense of your loss, then grab onto grief math.

The future without the love and example of my mother is uncertain, just as it has been since December 12, 1998. What I am sure of is that my mom died young, I proudly faced my grief and continue to do so, and she'll be forever frozen at 44 while I live past that age. Don't hide your grief, because it's how we say, "I love you and miss you."

Je t'aime, Maman. Tu me manques.

Acknowledgments

GIVEN THAT THIS BOOK COVERS 27 years of grief, my thank-yous will cover lots of people, places, and pets who are still active parts of my life and some who are no longer a part of my life, due to circumstances or death. Whatever their current role in my life may be, at some point, they had an impact on my ability to find hope in grief. They made me feel loved when I felt alone while using their tools to support me. They let me grieve without ever making me feel it was time to stop. We never stop grieving someone we love.

Thank you to those who were with me during the first years of grief math. Beebaw and Papa, thank you for loving my mom and changing her life. I am the luckiest "Sweetie Pie" to be your granddaughter. Paul Dudash, you checked on me when Dad was out of town and took great care of me as I started my career. Mom would be so grateful to you.

The Awty International School classes of 1999 and 2000 and Upper School faculty and staff, particularly the senior IB Theatre class and Mr. Clarke, Madame Crénault, and Bernardo Cubria: I survived each day and every 12th of the month because of the safe spaces you created for me to cry and feel seen at school. Bernardo, all of your uniform shirts had mascara stains on the shoulders because you let me cry as much as I needed. I often wonder how I would've handled each day of those first few months if you had not been by my side. Many schools would let a grieving student fall through the cracks, but Awty kept me surrounded by caring and kind people.

Susan Beers Sindhu, you flew from Germany for my high school graduation to represent Mom. I will never forget floating in the pool with you as you openly shared memories of Mom and your pain in losing her. Francine Webb and les Pinots de Villechenons, you gave both Mom and me a French home in both Houston and Paris. While you both changed my life by giving me summers as an exchange student with a loving family, you also helped fulfill Mom's Bucket List.

1990s Glendaloch Farm barn family and Crista Bandini, I don't know how I would've coped with the first year without you. You hosted my high school graduation party, were some of the first people to come to our house after Mom died, and you loved Dancer and me so deeply. Crista, you remain an important part of my life today, and your friendship is a beautiful gift.

Kelly Taylor Buerger, you were the first person to welcome me into the Motherless Daughters Club. Thank you for handing me the book that made me feel validated and heard.

Sweet Briar College: being surrounded by women who are thoughtful, compassionate, critical thinkers was exactly what I needed at such a crucial time. The Meakims, you gave me a home, family, and love when I needed it most. My sweet Virginia home was full of deep conversations on a suede couch, Italian hoagies, and mornings on the porch. I cannot ever truly thank you for the safe space and love you gave in your lovely spot along the James River.

Arnaud de Buyl, you never shied from talking about my mom and being the brother I needed in those early years. David Jancheski, you taught me more about my mom than I could have imagined. Your friendship with her was beautiful, and I pray you are painting together with the most beautiful colors.

Memorial Hermann Hospital-TMC's 2007–2008 CPE Residency group and supervisors: you taught me how to be the chaplain people needed and listened with such empathy. Abby, Mercedes, Claire, and Dancer: your love and companionship forever connected me to Mom and who I am.

— • —

GRIEF MATH GRATITUDE · AGES 34 TO 43

Thank you to those who were with me in the middle years. Aunt Peggy: our weekly post-*Downton Abbey* recaps and chats during my visits filled my soul. I miss you deeply.

The Dietitian Gals and PICU APPs who never left when so many others did. Geneva McBrayer, we bonded over our love for brave kids and a love for "an exemplary vegetable that is the potato." I'm sorry yet grateful that we share December 12. Thank you for being a grief partner, an encourager, and a wonderful friend.

Arsenal FC — including the supporters, staff, and players — you gave me a home and a place to belong. I feel it whether I'm singing and cheering from my couch or from the stands at the Emirates. While I have been a supporter since the 1990s, I truly felt part of the community in the last few years, and being part of the global Gooners has helped me understand what true community feels like.

*   ·   *

GRIEF MATH GRATITUDE · THE 44TH YEAR

Thank you to those who gave special care to me during the ultimate year of grief math, as I spent my 44th year in deep grief that felt incredibly similar to the first year. Hope Edelman and every Motherless Daughter I've met over the last 27 years — but particularly in 2025, in our community, including Carrie Walker Nettles, Terra Chamberlain, and Kelly Taylor Buerger: you gave me the community I needed when I was 17 and didn't have one.

My deepest gratitude goes to Active Riding Trips, Killarney Riding Stables, my riding buddies and guides, and every person we met at pubs, restaurants, hotels, B&Bs, and on the street along the Ring of Kerry who showed me the beauty of Ireland on my bucket list trip. Everyone who cheered me on as my daydream for this book became a reality made me believe I could do this, and I'm grateful.

*   ·   *

SPECIAL GRATITUDE · SŪTRA HOUSE

To the entire team at Sūtra House: you made editing and writing my first book a dream. Thank you for believing in my story and seeing the value in my manuscript. I felt encouraged and seen by your support, and I cannot thank you enough for guiding me into my author era.

——————— • ———————

MY DEEPEST GRATITUDE

To anyone who has ever told me a story about my mom or asked me to tell one: your stories and questions are healing.

Carrie Walker Nettles, you are the safest of spaces and my kindred spirit. You listen. You challenge me, and you inspire me. You see and hear me. Your friendship is a gift straight from our loving God.

Daisy and Lily, you taught me to breathe and explore. Buckley, you brought such love, tenderness, and awareness of the safe and scary parts of the world. You were my little buddy through the grief of the Big Three and some of the most difficult moments in my career, and you were the first true Shannerman.

Stewie, your curiosity and companionship are such a comfort in my grief. Like your brother Oliver, you are joy personified. And like Buckley, you kiss with abandon.

Oliver: you're my soul dog. You changed me. You taught me how to love, how to feel safe, and how to witness God's presence in the smallest things.

Gunner, you are an answered prayer. Every girl dreams of having a horse of her own, but few get one like you. You are my mirror, my boy. You have companioned me through the losses of the Texas Pups and much more. Every ride, every snuggle, every hand graze, and every little prayer we say together is felt in my soul. I will love and protect you for your whole life, just as you've watched me do with your canine siblings.

I am a better person for being the dog mom and horse mom to Oliver, Buckley, Stewie, Lily, Daisy, and Gunner, and I couldn't have coped with chaplaincy or personal grief without them.

Patrick: I never had anyone truly in my corner until you were a part of my life. You are my advocate, my partner in all things, and my favorite human. I am incredibly proud of all you've accomplished. There's no one with whom I'd rather raise dogs.

EVERY STORY, A THREAD.

www.ingramcontent.com/pod-product-compliance
Lightning Source LLC
Chambersburg PA
CBHW020915060726
47591CB00004B/1250